Eyewitness
PREDATOR

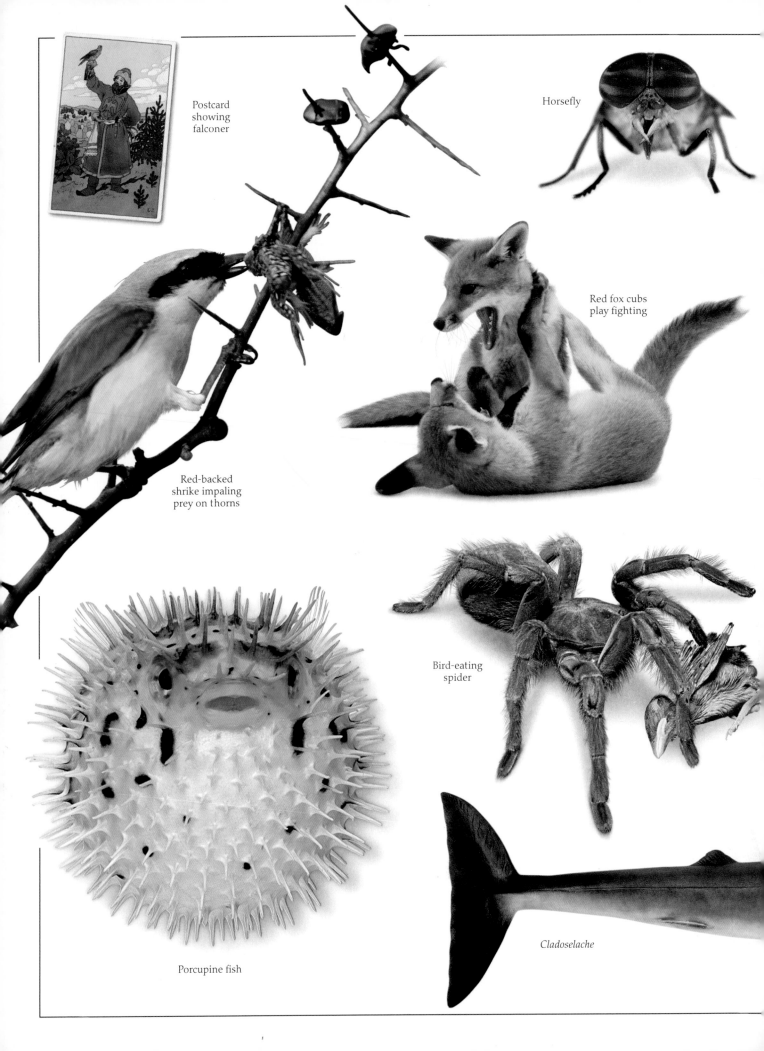

Postcard
showing
falconer

Horsefly

Red-backed
shrike impaling
prey on thorns

Red fox cubs
play fighting

Bird-eating
spider

Porcupine fish

Cladoselache

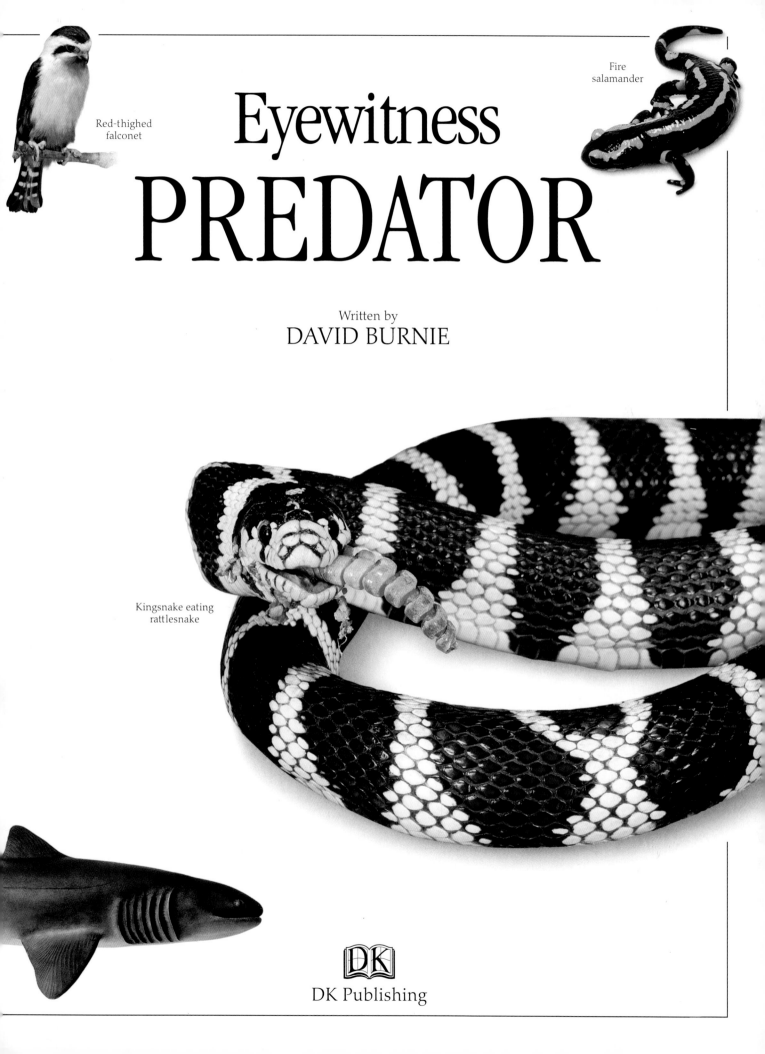

Red-thighed
falconet

Fire
salamander

Eyewitness
PREDATOR

Written by
DAVID BURNIE

Kingsnake eating
rattlesnake

DK
DK Publishing

Talon of a
red-shouldered
hawk

LONDON, NEW YORK,
MELBOURNE, MUNICH, AND DELHI

Consultant Dr. Kim Dennis-Bryan

DK DELHI

Project editor Kingshuk Ghoshal
Project art editor Govind Mittal
Assistant editor Bharti Bedi
Designers Deep Shikha Walia, Nitu Singh
Senior DTP designer Tarun Sharma
DTP designers Mohammad Usman,
Neeraj Bhatia, Nand Kishor
DTP manager Sunil Sharma
Managing editor Suchismita Banerjee
Managing art editor Romi Chakraborty
Production manager Pankaj Sharma

DK LONDON

Senior editor Dr. Rob Houston
Senior art editor Carol Davis
US editor Margaret Parrish
Associate publisher Andrew Macintyre
Picture researcher Jo Walton
Production editor Marc Staples
Production controller Charlotte Oliver
Jacket designer Neal Cobourne

First published in the United States in 2011
by DK Publishing, 375 Hudson Street, New York, New York 10014

Copyright © 2011 Dorling Kindersley Limited, London

10 9 8 7 6 5 4 3 2 1

001—178349—Jul/11

A catalog record for this book is available
from the Library of Congress.

ISBN 978-0-7566-8267-5 (Hardcover)
978-0-7566-8268-2 (Library binding)

Color reproduction by MDP, UK
Printed and bound by Toppan Printing Co. (Shenzhen) Ltd., China

www.dk.com

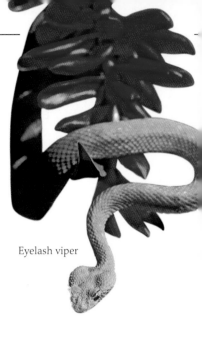

Eyelash viper

Blue-ringed
octopus

Deep-sea
angler fish

Skull of
Tengmalm's owl

Portrait of
pitcher plants

Chameleon
catching prey

Contents

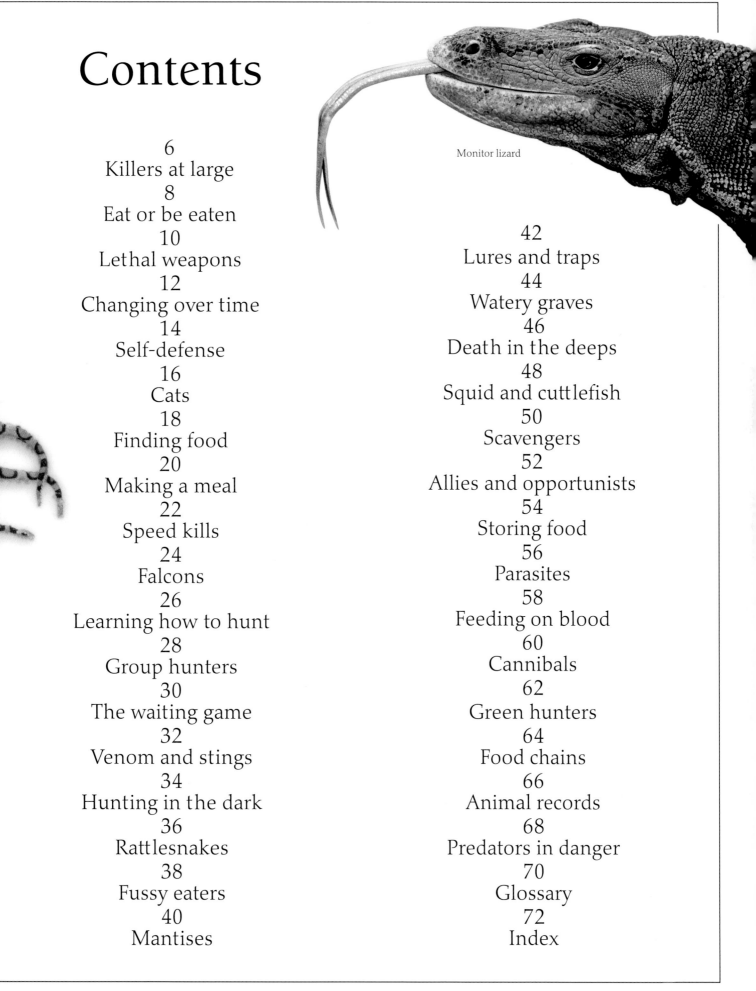

Monitor lizard

Killers at large

PREDATORS ARE BORN TO KILL. They feed by catching and eating other animals, which are known as their prey. Most predators hunt their prey one by one, but some eat on a gigantic scale, filtering food out of the water by the ton. In addition to true predators, many other animals have a predatory streak. They include omnivores with wide-ranging diets, as well as parasites, blood-feeders, and animals that scavenge dead remains. All these get their food wholly or partly from animals, but true predators are the only ones that must kill to survive.

TOP-LEVEL PREDATOR
Polar bear

3RD-LEVEL PREDATOR
Ringed seal

2ND-LEVEL PREDATOR
Polar cod

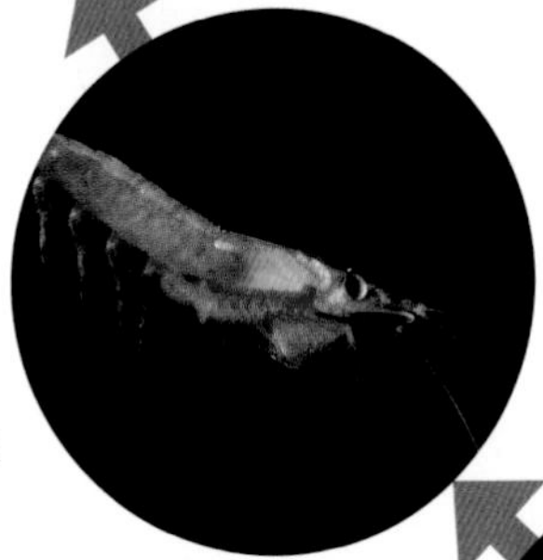

1ST-LEVEL PREDATOR
Northern krill

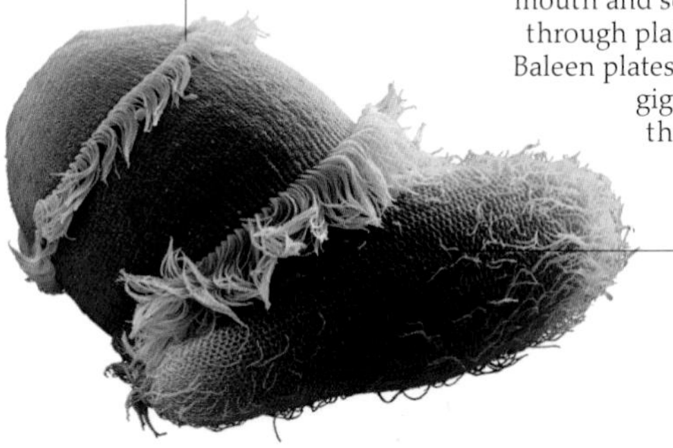

Ring of tiny hairs makes Didinium *spin through water*

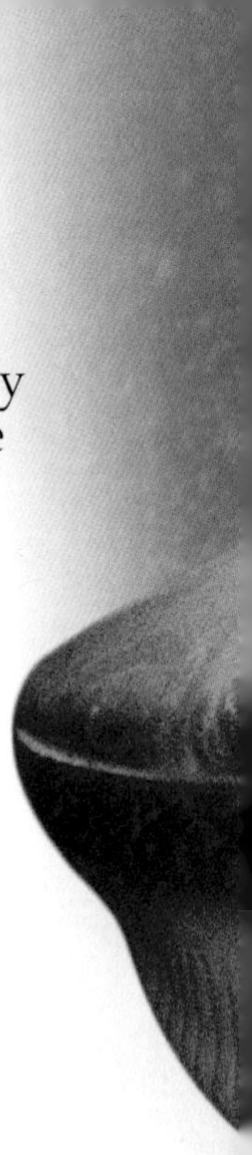

LIVING GIANTS
The biggest predator of all time is the blue whale, which can weigh more than 110 tons (100 metric tons). Instead of catching prey individually, it engulfs swarms of shrimplike krill with its gaping mouth, which expands like an enormous balloon. The whale then closes its mouth and squeezes its throat, forcing the water and krill through plates of baleen, which hang from its upper jaw. Baleen plates have frayed edges, making them work like a gigantic strainer. The plates trap the krill, which the whale then swallows, as the water escapes.

Paramecium—*another single-celled creature*

MICROPREDATORS
In the living world, microscopic predators far outnumber those that are visible to the naked eye. Some are tiny animals, while others are single-celled creatures that hunt down microscopic prey. Here, a single-celled *Didinium* is attacking a *Paramecium* in a pond. This predator has a simple mouthlike opening, but it does not have a throat or any internal organs. Instead, it simply engulfs its prey and then breaks down its food.

1ST-LEVEL CONSUMER
Copepod

LINKS IN A CHAIN
Predators are joined by invisible food chains, which show how energy and nutrients transfer when predators eat their prey. The chain shown here, from the Arctic, starts with phytoplankton (tiny plantlike plankton), which make food by utilizing the Sun's energy. They are the chain's producers. Copepods are small crustaceans that feed on these producers. The copepods are eaten by northern krill, the chain's first-level predators. The chain includes two more predators, until it reaches the polar bear, where it ends. The polar bear is a top predator because it has no natural enemies, once it has grown to adult size.

PRODUCER
Phytoplankton

Throat pleats tighten to force water out of mouth

OMNIVORES
Predators are not always full-time hunters. Many of them are omnivores, or animals that eat all kinds of food. Baboons often hunt, but they also eat fruit and seeds, while chimps, bears, and crows eat almost anything edible that they can find. Omnivores usually have keen senses and include some unusually quick-witted animals. Some kinds—such as raccoons and foxes—make a good living by feeding on waste humans throw away.

Bird louse gripping peafowl feather

PARASITES
Instead of eating prey, parasites use other animals as a long-term source of food. They live on or inside another animal, known as their host, and often feed by sucking blood or by absorbing semidigested food. Most parasites, including this bird louse, are smaller than the animals they attack and typically target a single kind of host. But parasites also include animals with complex life cycles, which target two or three very different hosts at different stages of their lives.

Baboon feeding on impala

SCAVENGERS
Some predators eat only food that they have killed themselves, and completely ignore dead remains. At the other extreme, vultures search out animal carcasses, and hardly ever kill anything themselves. Animals like these are known as scavengers. In the sea, scavengers include many animals that feed on drifting particles and dead remains. On land, they include animals ranging from beetles, which feed on dead skin and fur, to hyenas. Some scavengers, such as hyenas, are also capable hunters.

Eat or be eaten

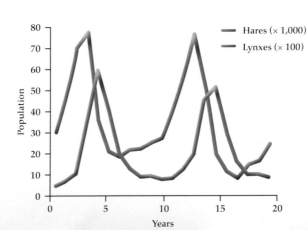

KILLING FOR A LIVING IS NOT EASY. It takes time and effort, and there is always the risk of being killed while on the hunt. But when hunger strikes, predators have no choice. They have to eat, even if it means gambling with their lives. Many predators are omnivores, or animals that eat a wide variety of food. Brown bears eat fruits, roots, fish, and even moths and beetle grubs. Hunters also scavenge. Spotted hyenas, for example, quickly gather at dead remains, in addition to hunting anything they can catch and kill. Predators also include specialists, such as the song thrush and Canadian lynx. They eat a narrow range of food, so if their prey goes through hard times, they do as well.

RECOGNIZING FOOD
Like many birds and mammals, the song thrush learns partly from its parents how to recognize its prey. It feeds on earthworms, and also on banded snails, which it breaks open by smashing against stones. It uses mental pictures, or search images, of its food. If an animal matches a search image, the thrush eats it. If not, the bird leaves it alone.

LINKED TOGETHER
The fortunes of predators are dependent on those of their prey. In the Canadian Arctic, the number of snowshoe hares rises and falls in natural cycles lasting about 10 years. These cycles are caused mainly by the supply of twigs, which the hares use as their winter food. In turn, Canadian lynxes depend on the hares for food. Their numbers rise and fall like the hares', but with a time-lag of about 3 or 4 years.

PICKING A VICTIM
Loping past a flock of flamingos, a spotted hyena searches for sick or injured birds. In this open habitat, it cannot attack by surprise, so it seeks out weak birds on the edge of the flock and grabs them before they can take off. Flamingos are almost completely defenseless, and they rely on constant vigilance to survive. But not all birds are like this. Some species—such as terns and gulls—retaliate furiously if they are attacked.

Graph: Population vs Years (0–20). Y-axis: Population (0–80). Legend: Hares (× 1,000), Lynxes (× 100).

Oldest chick

Middle chick

Unhatched egg

FOOD AND FAMILIES

When predators go hungry, their young face difficult times. With mammals and birds, the young are usually the same size, and they have an equal chance of getting enough food. Many predatory birds—such as this short-eared owl—have a different kind of family life. They usually lay 2–5 eggs, which hatch a few days apart. This means that the young differ in size. In good years, all the young survive, but in bad ones, the oldest chick gets the most or all of the food and at times may even eat the smaller ones!

RIGHT PLACE, RIGHT TIME

Successful predators have to be in the right place to catch their prey, often at the right time of year. In the fall, brown bears gather along rivers to catch salmon migrating upstream. They wade into rapids and then grab salmon as the fish jump through the air. This annual feast lasts several weeks, and the protein from it lets some bears reach weights of 1 ton. This is up to four times as much as brown bears that live far away from rivers, where there are no fish to eat.

UNWELCOME INVADERS

For thousands of years, humans have accidentally or deliberately carried predatory mammals around the world. On remote islands—big and small—foxes, cats, stoats, and rats have had a huge impact, driving many local animals to the edge of extinction. Red foxes are particularly adaptable invaders. Unlike cats, they have a wide-ranging diet that includes small mammals, birds, and insects, as well as plant food.

Fang is
hidden inside
sheath of skin

Elastic
ligaments
allow room
for stretching

Lethal weapons

ALL PREDATORS HAVE TOOLS that help them catch and kill their prey. These include different body parts, from teeth and beaks to pincers and crushing claws. They also include substances made by predators' bodies, such as poisons, silk, and sticky slime. In addition to catching and killing, these weapons often protect their owners, by reducing the chance of them being harmed by their prey. To be effective, animal weapons have to be maintained. Many of them grow constantly, keeping them sharp, while others are replaced. But not all animals have renewable weapons. Predatory mammals, including wolves, usually have just one set of adult teeth. They have to last for life.

OPEN WIDE
Many predators have hinged jaws, which they use to attack their prey. A puff adder's jaws are made of bone, like human ones, but their unusually loose hinges give them an enormous gape (wide stretch). The upper and lower jaw and their left and right sides are joined by flexible ligaments, which stretch like strong rubber bands. These allow the snake to swallow prey bigger than its head. The puff adder is one of the world's most poisonous snakes, with a dangerous habit of lying in wait on paths.

Incisor helps
to bite prey

KILLING KIT
With its mouth wide open in a yawn, a gray wolf displays its impressive teeth. Like all mammalian carnivores, it has a varied set of teeth, including incisors that nip, canines that grip, and carnassials that crush and slice. Many other predators, including crocodiles and many fish, have simpler teeth that are replaced all the time. A crocodile can get through 3,000 teeth in its lifetime, while an adult wolf has just 42 permanent teeth that are preceded by baby teeth.

Carnassial helps to
slice through flesh of prey

Daggerlike
canine helps
to grip prey

DEATH TRAP
With its jaws open in a straight line, a trapjaw ant looms over its aphid prey. Like all insects, it has jaws made of chitin—the same material that covers the rest of its body. Its jaws open and close sideways, instead of up and down, and they have jagged inner edges, and lethal hook-shaped tips. To kill prey, they snap shut in just over 150 millionths of a second—one of the fastest movements in the animal world.

Trapjaw ant

Sharp toothlike
knob, or tubercle,
increases grip
on fish or other
slippery prey

CRUSHING AND CUTTING
Lobsters are armed with reinforced claws, which they use for self-defense and for killing prey. When a lobster is young, its claws are the same size and shape, but they develop differently as it grows up. One claw becomes much heavier than the other and is used for crushing food and cracking open shells. Its partner, known as a pincer, is flatter, and has a sharper inside edge. The lobster uses this to grab and cut up soft-bodied prey.

*Toe's scaly skin
helps to grip prey*

*Talon keeps
growing to
make up for
wear and tear*

TALONS

Birds of prey attack
their prey feet-first.
Their toes are armed with
sharp claws, or talons, which
grip and kill their prey. These
talons are of a red-shouldered
hawk. Their curved shape makes
them pierce the prey when the toes
close, and they also let the hawk carry
its prey back to its nest. A red-shouldered hawk's talons
are about ¾ in (2 cm) long. The largest talons belong
to the American harpy eagle. Measuring up to 2½ in
(6.5 cm) long, they can kill adult monkeys and sloths.

Gray heron
with a fish
in its beak

STAB AND SWALLOW

Birds do not have teeth—instead,
most predatory kinds, other than
birds of prey, use their beaks to catch
and kill their food. This gray heron
has successfully speared a fish and
will flick it into the air, so that it drops
head-first down its throat. Birds' beaks
are made of bone covered with a layer
of keratin—the same substance found
in hooves and hair. The tips and sides
are packed with nerves. Some birds,
such as curlews, use these to hunt
by touch alone.

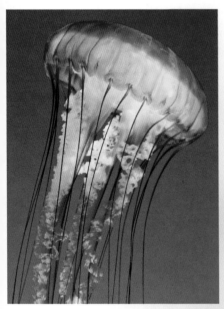

MICROSTINGS

Many animals use poisons for self-defense,
but jellyfish use them to stun or kill their
prey. Their tentacles are armed with huge
numbers of nematocysts, or microstings,
which fire the moment another animal
comes within close range. Each nematocyst
shoots out a poison-tipped thread, stabbing
it into the jellyfish's prey. Nematocysts are
dangerous because they work automatically.
They continue to fire as long as a jellyfish
is wet, which is why it is dangerous to
touch jellyfish washed up on the shore.

Changing over time

Caption: Kea feeding on a dead hare

EVER SINCE LIFE FIRST APPEARED ON EARTH, living things have gradually evolved. Evolution is the process of change by which animals, plants, and other living organisms adapt to a changing environment over many generations, passing on the features that help the organisms to survive better. Predators have evolved new shapes and new ways of hunting prey. At the same time, prey animals have evolved new defenses. Animal evolution takes place over a long period, which makes it hard to see in action. However, it leaves a rich trail of evidence, which is built into every form of life. Biologists first began studying evolution in the 19th century. At first, they noticed evolution by comparing the shapes of fossils with living things. Gradually, they discovered the driving forces behind evolution, which include natural selection, and the way living things pass on features to their offspring. Today, scientists can study evolution with great precision. They can trace the path that evolution has followed, and find out how closely different kinds of life are related.

HOW EVOLUTION OCCURS
Evolution occurs in several ways. One of the most important is through natural selection. Individuals with features that give them a better chance of survival have more young that survive. Some of these young inherit those features, and their features become more widespread. Parrots, for example, have hooked beaks, and most, including the scarlet macaw, feed on plants. But in New Zealand, where there are no native predatory mammals, a parrot called the kea evolved an extra-long predator's beak. This special feature lets it hunt animals.

Caption: Scarlet macaw

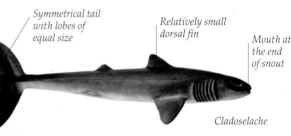

Symmetrical tail with lobes of equal size

Relatively small dorsal fin

Mouth at the end of snout

Cladoselache

PREDATORS FROM THE PAST
Fossils are like a window on the past, showing what prehistoric life was like, and how predators and prey have evolved. *Cladoselache*, for example, was a distant relative of modern sharks and lived more than 360 million years ago. It shared the same ancestor as living sharks, but it had several features that set it apart from modern kinds. Its mouth was at the front of its head, instead of underneath, and its skin was smooth, instead of being covered with denticles, or rough scales.

Asymmetrical tail with large upper lobe and small lower lobe

Large dorsal fin

Great white shark

Mouth on underside, to the rear of snout

END OF THE LINE

Evolution has produced millions of new species during the history of life on Earth. At the same time, many others have died out, or become extinct. These extinct species include some of the world's most successful predators, which are known only from fossil remains. Among them are ammonites—shelled relatives of octopuses and squid, which lived in the seas for over 350 million years. The ammonite shown here, called *Scaphites*, was one of the last members in this highly successful line. It died out in the same wave of extinctions that killed the dinosaurs.

Spinosaurus

GOING TO EXTREMES

Evolution does not move in any set direction. If conditions are stable, some animals may stay the same for millions of years. However, predators often grow larger during evolution, and sometimes evolve to extreme sizes. In the past, some meat-eating dinosaurs became gigantic creatures, the heaviest predators ever to have lived on land. *Spinosaurus* probably weighed more than 13 tons (12 metric tons), making it even larger than *Tyrannosaurus rex*. It may have stalked the banks of rivers and lakes, using its crocodilelike jaws to catch fish.

Least weasel

WHEN SMALL IS BETTER

Being smaller sometimes gives predators a better chance of survival. One example of this is the least weasel, a tiny mammalian carnivore not much thicker than a finger. It pursues rodents into their burrows, although it can also kill rabbits three or four times its own size. Other examples of miniature predators include thread snakes, which can be just 4 in (10 cm) long, and falconets, the world's smallest birds of prey. All of them have evolved from larger species, instead of the other way around.

Rough-skinned newt

Common garter snake

EVOLVING TOGETHER

In nature, two or more organisms may evolve together, triggering changes in each other in a process called co-evolution. Between predator and prey, co-evolution can produce a biological arms race, as each species constantly adapts to an evolving adversary. This kind of arms race has happened between the rough-skinned newt and the common garter snake. The newt has toxins, or poisons, that repel its predator, but the snake has become partially immune to them. In response, the newt has become more toxic, but the snake's immunity has increased as well.

Self-defense

IF A PREDATOR THREATENS TO ATTACK, most animals escape as fast as they can. Given a good head start, this straightforward method of self-defense often saves their lives, but there is always a chance that the predator will catch up and make a kill. Many prey animals avoid this risk, because they have evolved different kinds of self-defense. Some use camouflage to keep from being seen, but others make no attempt to hide. Their vivid markings show that they have special protection, making them difficult or dangerous to eat. Some animals use even stranger tactics—they fall down and pretend to be dead. Most predators attack only prey that moves, so this extreme tactic often saves lives.

Outer casing of the insect has a barklike texture

MAKE BELIEVE
Insects have countless predators, from frogs and lizards to birds. For many of them, camouflage (blending in with their backgrounds) is the key to survival. Some insects simply camouflage themselves, but others—including this stick insect—imitate inedible objects with amazing precision. Stick insects sway gently when they move, resembling twigs blowing in the breeze. It is difficult for a predator to recognize them, or to tell their head from their tail.

Hair can irritate skin or mucus glands of a predator

BRISTLING ARMORY
Caterpillars cannot run from predators, but they are often protected in other ways. This lappet moth caterpillar is covered with ultrafine hairs, which can trigger violent allergies in humans. The hairs can cause temporary blindness if they come into contact with a predator's eyes, and painful rashes if they touch bare skin. Both effects can last for days.

BACKING INTO DANGER
Caught out in the open by a lion, a crested porcupine turns its back on its enemy and raises the sharply pointed quills on its back. It rattles the blunt-tipped quills on its tail, showing that it is preparing to counterattack. If the lion does not back away, the porcupine goes into action. Suddenly reversing, it jabs dozens of quills into its enemy's muzzle and leaves them embedded in its skin. Once in place, the quills can cause serious infections, and even death.

PLAYING DEAD
With its mouth open and its body inert, a grass snake shows no signs of being alive. This bizarre form of self-defense—known as thanatosis—works because most predators hunt moving prey. If their prey suddenly stops moving, their hunting instincts are switched off, and they lose interest and move on. Thanatosis has evolved in a wide range of animals, from insects to frogs and mammals. Some animals will not move even if touched.

Spine pointing outward provides second line of defense

Limp tongue aids in pretense

TOUCH ME NOT
Fire salamanders move very slowly, making them easy to catch. However, their bold colors are a clear warning sign, telling would-be predators not to come too close. Their rubbery skin is protected by poisonous secretions, and glands behind their eyes can spray poison up to 6 ft (2 m) into the air. No two fire salamanders have exactly the same skin pattern. Some have yellow spots, while others have broad yellow stripes. But in all of them the message is the same—keep clear, or risk a poisonous counterattack.

WATERLOGGED
If threatened, a porcupine fish gulps in water, making its stomach swell up like a balloon. At the same time, its long spines hinge outward, making the fish almost impossible to eat. Fully inflated, a porcupine fish can barely swim. It tumbles around helplessly if touched, but once the danger has passed, it deflates and returns to its normal size.

Quill on back has shallow roots, and detaches easily

SAFE SURROUNDINGS
Clownfish have few defenses of their own, but they have powerful allies. They form lifelong partnerships with giant sea anemones, and retreat into their tentacles at the first sign of danger. For most fish, this would be deadly, because the tentacles of sea anemones are armed with microscopic stings. However, clownfish are covered by a layer of external slime, which protects them from their hosts. Scientists are unsure exactly how the slime works. It may stop the anemone's stings from firing as the fish brushes past.

Cats

CATS MAKE UP ONE OF THE most distinctive groups of mammalian predators. The first cat appeared about 20 million years ago. Many different species have evolved from this ancestor. They include today's living cats, as well as dozens of kinds—such as saber-toothed cats—which lived in prehistoric times. Cats are almost entirely carnivorous, and apart from lions, almost all are solitary hunters, relying on their retractable claws and canine teeth to catch and kill their prey. Some of the largest species can be dangerous to humans and livestock. However, the domestic cat is one of the world's most widespread mammalian predators—largely due to its association with people and its ability to become feral, reverting to life in the wild.

A SHARED SHAPE

Today, there are about 36 species in the cat family, ranging in size from a tiger to the African black-footed cat, which is only 8 in (20 cm) high. Despite their differences in size, all have similarly shaped skulls, with forward-facing eyes and short but powerful jaws. They have four canine teeth and blade-edged cheek teeth, or carnassials, which slice up their food. Their tongues are covered with backward-pointing spines, or papillae, which they use to scrape food off carcasses and to groom their fur.

Tongue covered with rough papillae

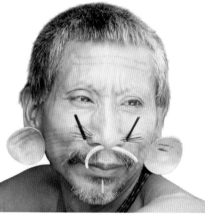

CATS IN MYTHOLOGY

Cats play a part in many traditions and mythologies, being feared, admired, or revered. This Amazonian hunter is wearing traditional jaguar decorations that are thought to confer prowess and success. In the Maya civilization of Central America, the jaguar was a symbol of power and connection with the afterlife, while in ancient Egypt, the domestic cat was revered. Thousands were mummified after death and placed in special tombs.

Large canine tooth stabs prey

Tiger

Heavy lower jaw withstands pressure of a powerful bite

FABULOUS FUR

Fur keeps cats warm and provides them with camouflage for hunting by stealth. Some cats—such as the pumas and lions—are a plain brown, but many, including the clouded leopard, are beautifully marked with stripes, spots, rosettes, or irregular cloudlike marks. These markings are present in the outer coat of long guard hairs. Beneath this is an undercoat of soft, fine wool. The guard hairs are water-repellent, so the wool beneath rarely gets wet, even in heavy rain.

LISTEN AND LEAP

Many small cats hunt by listening for their prey, before pouncing on it with extraordinary agility and precision. This serval—a long-legged cat from Africa—can leap up to 13 ft (4 m) horizontally, landing on its prey with enough force to stun the animal. It uses its front paws to pin its prey to the ground and then grabs the prey in its jaws. Cats are also very good at twisting movements of the spine. The caracal, a small cat from Africa and Asia, uses this to leap upward and knock birds out of the air.

Clouded leopard

CAT CLUB

Unlike other cats, lions are social animals. They live together in family groups called prides, containing about a dozen lionesses and their cubs, and often a pair of adult males. Pride members nuzzle and rub each other to exchange a shared scent, which acts as an identity badge. Mothers frequently lick and groom each other and their offspring.

HUNTING AND FEEDING

Helped by her three cubs, a female cheetah finishes the remains of an antelope that she has killed. Cheetahs are unusual cats, because they hunt largely by sight. They run down their prey in the open without making any attempt to hide. Most other cats hunt by stealth, and use hearing and smell as well as vision to track down their prey. Apart from cheetahs, most cats stalk their prey at dusk and after dark. Like many mammalian carnivores, they have a reflective layer behind their eyes, which improves their vision when the light level is low.

Finding food

IT IS HARD TO IMAGINE WHAT IT IS LIKE to see through eyes that move independently, or to be able to sense animals' living electricity. But for some predators, feats like these are routine. Predators depend on their senses to find food. These senses depend on their habitats, their prey, and the way they have evolved. For many land-based predators, vision is the most vital sense, particularly when the prey is on the move. Smell, taste, and hearing are also important for predatory mammals and reptiles, while insects and other invertebrates often hunt by touch. Most fish can sense the scent of food, but sharks can also detect weak electrical fields produced by living things. This guides them to hidden prey, buried in the seabed.

Tiny black pits called ampullae of Lorenzini

Shape of head helps to spread ampullae, giving shark an accurate fix on prey

Pinhole-shaped pupil produces a sharply focused image over a wide range of distances

ELECTRICAL SWEEP
With their bizarre head flaps, hammerhead sharks are some of the strangest-looking predators in the seas. Like all sharks, they have special sense organs, called ampullae of Lorenzini. These are concentrated in their snouts, and in the flat wings on either side of their head. Hammerhead sharks usually feed on the seabed. The ampullae sense the slightest electrical disturbances created by the muscle movement of fish, letting the sharks find prey they cannot see.

ALL-SEEING EYES
Staring straight ahead through its turret-shaped eyes, a chameleon can catch an insect using its extendable tongue. Chameleons are the only lizards that can direct their eyes forward, and this helps them to judge the exact distance to their prey. At other times, their eyes swivel independently, so they can look in two completely different directions at the same time as they search for prey.

THE SCENT OF FOOD
Of all predatory mammals, bears have one of the keenest senses of smell. Polar bears feed mainly on seals and can smell them through 3 ft (1 m) of hardened snow, or across half a mile (1 km) of ice. This is amazing for any predator, but it is even more remarkable in subzero conditions. Airborne scents have to evaporate (turn to gas) before they enter the nose. The colder it is, the less scent gets airborne, so the less there is for a predator to smell.

Scent molecules stick to lizard's tongue as it flicks through the air

TASTING THE AIR
Monitor lizards taste the air for the scent of food by flicking their tongues out. Snakes also use this method of smelling, helping them to avoid predators and track down their prey. The process works in two steps. First, the tongue collects scent molecules from the air. The animal then pulls in its tongue, and presses the two tips into the roof of its mouth. There, nerve-lined hollows, which make up the Jacobson's organ, then sense the molecules, sending signals to the animal's brain.

TRACKING BY SOUND
Foxes have a good sense of smell, but they can also hunt by listening for their prey. For Arctic foxes, this is particularly important in winter, because the lemmings that they eat are hidden beneath the snow. Arctic foxes trot over the snowfields until they hear lemmings on the move below. Keeping quite still, a fox listens carefully to pinpoint its prey, before leaping with a catlike pounce to make a kill.

Front leg used for sensing prey

THE LETHAL TOUCH
Many small predators use the sense of touch to hunt on the ground, underneath it, or on the seabed. Some have sensitive antennae, but whip spiders feel for prey using a pair of extremely long front legs, moving sideways across the ground. If they touch anything edible, they seize it with their spiny pedipalps—feelers near the mouth—which fold shut to grip and kill.

Pedipalp

SENSING VIBRATIONS
When flying insects crash-land in water, predators soon appear on the scene. Some of the first predators to arrive are pondskaters—carnivorous bugs that can walk on the water surface with water-repellent feet. They have piercing mouthparts and feed by sucking up the body fluids of the prey. When their feet—the sense organs—detect ripples from an insect struggling on water, they quickly row toward it and start to eat.

Long leg of pondskater senses rapid vibrations produced by struggling insects

Making a meal

Food exchanged by wood ants

PREDATORS NEED FOOD to get energy, but their eating styles vary, as does the length of time they can last without food. Some insects and spiders can go for a year without eating. Being cold-blooded, or ectothermic, their bodies need little energy, except for when they breed. Many other cold-blooded predators eat more often, either because they are bigger, or because they spend more time on the move. Even so, a meal often lasts them for weeks or days. Birds and mammals need far more energy because they are warm-blooded, or endothermic. Some large predatory mammals, such as bears, can live off their body fat during winter, but small hunters have to hunt around the clock.

PASSING ON FOOD

Predators that live in groups usually feed themselves, except when they are raising young. But some animals—such as ants and wasps—work in a different way. Adult workers collect food and pass it on, so that it eventually reaches all the members of the nest. This kind of behavior is unusual in other predators. The only adult mammals known to do it are some carnivores, such as wolves and vampire bats, which regurgitate (eject contents from the stomach to the mouth) blood for hungry neighbors in their roosts.

FRANTIC FEEDERS

Grappling with an earthworm, a pygmy shrew looks too small for such large prey. However, this tiny but hyperactive hunter has sharply pointed teeth that let it kill and cut up animals its own size. Pygmy shrews are some of the world's smallest mammals, weighing just a quarter of a mouse. They have to eat their own weight in food every day. Without food, they can die in just three hours.

GIANT MEAL

With its jaws gaping wide, an African rock python slowly swallows an impala, which it has killed by squeezing in its coils. This giant snake—one of the world's largest—can swallow animals weighing up to 110 lb (50 kg). The snake takes several weeks to digest its enormous meal, but the process is extremely thorough, breaking down not only the flesh, but also the impala's horns, skin, and bones. After such a large meal, the python may not eat again for six months.

WRAPAROUND STOMACH

Starfish are slow-motion predators that creep over their prey. To eat, they push their stomachs outward through their mouths, and wrap them around their food. The stomach gradually digests the prey, letting the starfish absorb its meal. This starfish has turned upside down while feeding on a sea urchin. The folds of its stomach are still attached to its food, surrounded by rows of tube feet that the starfish uses to move.

Fur and bones of prey animals are matted together when pellet is dry

Fur mixed with mucus forms the glue that binds pellet

Skull of a prey animal

Hip bone of a prey animal with sockets for leg joint

LIQUIDS ONLY

This bird-eating spider is nearly 12 in (30 cm) across, but its mouth is so small that it can only swallow liquid food. Like all spiders, it digests its food by injecting the prey with enzymes. These dissolve the victim's organs, turning them into a nutritious soup that the spider then sucks up. During the breeding season, female spiders eat more than usual, because they put a large amount of energy into making eggs.

WASTE DISPOSAL

Once a predator has digested its prey, it gets rid of unwanted waste, such as bones, pieces of feathers, or other hard body parts. Most predators dispose of these in their droppings, but predatory birds often regurgitate them, in matted lumps called pellets. The pieces of a pellet shown here come from a barn owl roost. The bones inside it help to show what the owl has been hunting.

Speed kills

Predators have two main ways of catching food. Some hide and wait for prey to come their way, while others use speed to make a kill. Sitting and waiting uses much less energy, but high-speed predators usually manage to get more food. Some speedy hunters patiently stalk their prey, before launching a sudden attack. But in open habitats, where stalking is difficult, the world's fastest animals rely on quick bursts of speed to overtake their prey. These bursts push their bodies to their limits, which is why no hunter works at peak performance for long. Once they have caught food, many high-speed hunters slow down, but still eat on the move. Others—including the cheetah—stop entirely. Exhausted by the chase, they have to recover before they can start to feed.

Wing is stiff and slender, with a sharply pointed tip

AIR ACE
The alpine swift and its relatives are the fastest-moving predators in level flight. They often fly at more than 60 mph (100 kph), and some can reach 105 mph (170 kph) in short bursts, helped by highly streamlined bodies and thin, crescent-shaped wings. Swifts feed on insects, and they spend their whole lives in the air, except when they land to breed. They feed their young by filling their mouths with insects, using saliva to mix them into sticky balls.

Tail acts like a rudder to steer through sharp turns

Extra legs are added when the animal molts (sheds its outer casing)

MANY-LEGGED DASH
Except for flying insects, most invertebrates have low top speeds. But because many of them are small and light, they can gain speed rapidly from a standing start. On land, the house centipede is one of the fastest, running on long, slender legs. House centipedes feed on spiders and other small animals, and they often hunt indoors. At full speed, they can cover up to 20 in (50 cm) per second, as they run after their prey.

LETHAL PURSUIT
As its prey makes a desperate swerve, a cheetah closes in on a gazelle. The cheetah is the fastest land-based predator alive today, and perhaps the fastest runner of all time. Over short distances, it can reach speeds of 70 mph (112 kph), thanks to how efficiently its body uses energy to run, as well as its unusually flexible spine. Unlike most cats, which hunt by pouncing, it hunts by tripping its prey, using the sharp dew claw on each of its front paws.

Dorsal fin folds along the groove when fish swims _____

POWER SURGE

Sailfish can reach over 60 mph (100 kph)—about twice as fast as most speedboats, and 12 times faster than the Olympic swimming record. These spear-snouted predators have muscle-packed bodies and a stiff, scythelike tail that drives them through the sea. Sailfish prey on other fish in open water. They normally keep their sail-like dorsal fin folded away, but they can raise it to frighten their prey into a tight group, making them easier to attack.

Tail is held stiffly when swimming rapidly

Long, narrow fin has low drag, allowing fast, efficient swimming

Body is streamlined

Elongated bill helps to impale prey

FOUR-WINGED FLIGHT

Among predatory insects, dragonflies are some of the fastest in the air. Flying on two pairs of stiff, transparent wings, they can reach 34 mph (55 kph). They can hover or even reverse. Dragonflies use their bristly legs to snatch other flying insects, but they have two methods of hunting. Some wait on a perch and dart out when insects fly past. Others patrol over the ground, or over ponds and lakes, speeding after any insects that they spot with their extra-large eyes.

RIPPLE EFFECT

Dolphins are marine mammals, with streamlined bodies and special skin that helps them to swim at high speed. The outermost skin layer may flake away to be replaced every two hours, ensuring a smooth body surface that reduces drag, helping a dolphin to race after its prey. Most dolphins have a top speed of over 18 mph (30 kph). Some kinds often swim in front of ships—an easy way of traveling because a ship's bow wave gives them an extra push. This bottlenose dolphin is swimming close to the ocean floor and has grabbed an octopus in its tooth-filled jaws.

Cheetah chasing a gazelle

Falcons

SLENDER BODIES AND TAPERING wings make falcons supremely agile predators. They include the peregrine falcon—the world's fastest skydiving bird, as well as kestrels, pygmy falcons, and falconets, which are the smallest birds of prey. Falcons and their relatives have sharp talons, used for catching their food, and hooked beaks, which tear up anything that is too big to be swallowed whole. These birds have a range of attack techniques, which vary according to their prey. Some of the largest falcons attack other birds, snatching or wounding them in midair. Others prey on small mammals, reptiles, and insects, watching from a perch and then swooping onto their prey. Kestrels do this, too, but they also spot their prey by hovering and watching for signs of movement on the ground below.

FALCONS IN HISTORY
Falcons have a special place in the art of ancient Egypt. The Egyptians believed that the sky god, Horus, had the head of a falcon and the body of a man. Falcon heads often appeared in decorative wear—this example, from a necklace, is over 2,500 years old. Falcons also featured in pottery and in hieroglyphics, a form of writing that used images instead of an alphabet.

DANGER OVERHEAD
Common kestrels are experts at hovering—a way of flying normally found in much smaller birds. These brown and gray falcons often stay rock-steady at a height of about 33 ft (10 m), with their heads facing into the wind. Using their superb eyesight, they scan the ground for small animals, dropping silently, in stages, to make a kill. Common kestrels feed on a variety of animals, from mice to beetles, as well as on small birds and insects that they catch in midair.

Eye surrounded by brightly colored ring of skin

FEATURES OF A FALCON
There are nearly 40 species of falcon, and most—including this lanner falcon—have sleek, striped faces, and narrow, hooked beaks. Like all birds of prey, their eyes are good at picking out detail, and they face partly forward, giving falcons 3-D vision. Male falcons are usually smaller than the females, and sometimes live on different prey, thereby avoiding direct competition with their partners.

Wingspan is about 3¼–3½ ft (1–1.1 m)

Thin, tapered wing helps falcon to change direction quickly in flight

Sequence showing a peregrine falcon diving through air to attack prey

HIGH DIVER
Found all around the world, from the Arctic to Australia, the peregrine falcon attacks other birds in a steep dive, or stoop. During the stoop, it pursues its prey like a fighter plane, folding its wings as it hurtles toward the ground. Helped by gravity, it reaches speeds of up to 186 mph (300 kph)—the fastest speed of any animal on Earth. As it overtakes its prey, it slashes the prey with its talons, before returning to catch it and carry it to the ground. Peregrines often prey on pigeons, but they are highly selective feeders, eating the breast meat and leaving the rest of the corpse.

*Wing flutters
rapidly to keep bird
exactly over one spot*

*Tail spread out
and downward
to deflect wind*

*Foot held
close to
body during
dive*

*Tip of beak
notched, helping
to sever spine of
prey at its neck*

Russian postcard
showing a falconer
and falcon

*Wing held back
stiffly in a stoop*

FALCONRY
Trained falcons have been used for hunting
and sport since ancient times. Birds are
raised in captivity and taught to return to the
falconer after attacking their prey. The falconer
wears a protective glove, or gauntlet, and
the bird wears a leather hood when it is being
moved. Falconers work with a variety of birds,
aside from falcons. These include buzzards
and hawks, and sometimes eagles—the
world's largest raptors, or birds of prey.

*Sharp talon
slices prey in
midair*

BIG AND SMALL
The gyrfalcon is the largest species in the
falcon family. Females have a wingspan
of up to 5½ ft (1.6 m), and can weigh
4½ lb (2 kg)—about one-third more
than the males. These powerful
hunters feed on birds up to the
size of geese, and mammals such
as hares. They breed in rocky
places in the Arctic and have
variable plumage, ranging from
gray and dark brown to almost
white. At the other extreme,
falconets are the world's smallest
birds of prey, measuring about
6 in (15 cm) long. They live in the
forests of Southeast Asia and
feed mainly on flying insects.

RAISING YOUNG
Most falcons nest on their own, laying 2–5 eggs each
time they breed. Both parents usually take care of the
young. Here, an adult common kestrel has returned
to the nest with food. Young kestrels stay in the
nest for about a month. They shed their fluffy gray
plumage and replace it with a new set of feathers
so that they can fly.

Red-thighed
falconet

White
gyrfalcon

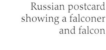

Learning how to hunt

FROM THE MOMENT IT IS BORN, a snake or shark knows how to hunt, even though it has never seen prey before. Many predators are the same. Their hunting behavior is instinctive, although they often get better at hunting with experience. Birds and mammals are different. Predatory ones inherit some hunting instincts, but learning plays a key role in their lives. By observing their parents, they gradually learn all about hunting, so that they can feed themselves and raise young of their own. There are many aspects to hunting. For some birds and mammals, acquiring these skills may take many months.

WATCH THIS
With an attentive stare, this young meerkat watches an adult eating a scorpion, which it has caught during a hunt. Meerkats hunt in gangs of up to 50 animals, and they eat a wide range of prey, from insects and scorpions, to lizards, mice, and birds. Each kind of food requires a different hunting technique—particularly scorpions that can fight back with a dangerous sting. Adults show young meerkats how to grab scorpions and bite off their stings, turning them into a harmless meal.

AIR TRAINING
Birds of prey give lessons to their fledglings to help them learn hunting skills. Most species—including this Steller's sea eagle—start the lessons in the nest, showing the young how to tear up food with their beaks. When the young leave the nest, training includes flight skills and prey capture, with the adults sometimes dropping food through the air for their young to catch. Steller's sea eagles take up to six months to learn how to hunt on their own.

Mother watches over cubs

PRACTICE MAKES PERFECT
At six months old, these cheetah cubs are practicing the serious business of making a kill. Their victim is a young gazelle, which their mother has caught and released. As the gazelle staggers to its feet, one of the cubs leaps on it, while the others rush to catch up. At this age, the cheetahs are not fast enough for high-speed hunts, but they practice many hunting moves, including tripping prey with the front paw. Between the ages of 12 and 18 months, the cubs become fully grown, and capable of killing adult antelope themselves.

TAKING THE PLUNGE
Most otters are born on land, but their food comes from rivers or the sea. When the young leave their den for the first time, they already know how to swim, but they are often reluctant to leave land. If this happens, their mother waits at the water's edge and encourages them to take the plunge. These young marine otters, from the coast of Peru, are now familiar with the sea and fully at home on the rocks and in the waves.

Red fox cubs
play fighting

LEARNING ON THE JOB
Unlike birds and mammals, octopuses grow up on
their own. This means that they do not learn to
hunt by mimicking their parents. Instead, they
use instinct, learning, and insight—the kind
of problem-solving that humans often use.
Here, an octopus is trying to reach a crab
from the safety of a pot. The crab is inside
a jar, but the octopus has figured out
how to unscrew the lid to get at its prey.

PLAYTIME
For young mammalian carnivores—including
these red foxes—play is a key part of growing
up. It prepares their bodies for hunting, and
also gives them social skills they need in later
life, when they may need to fight for a territory
or for the right to mate. Play fights may look
alarming, particularly among larger carnivores
such as bears, but they work to a strict set of
rules that ensures that little or no harm is done.
In a play fight, jaws are never fully closed while
biting, and the play fight ends when the losing
animal gives way—usually by lying on its back.

BITTER EXPERIENCE
The living world is full of animals that taste bad, or that
can retaliate if attacked. Predators recognize some of them
by instinct, but they have to learn about others by trial and
error. The monarch butterfly is one insect that birds learn to
avoid. It often contains poisons that its caterpillars collect from
milkweed plants, giving it a horrible taste. Blue jays soon learn
this if they eat a monarch butterfly, because it promptly makes
them sick. From then on, they avoid all monarch butterflies,
including those that actually contain no poison at all.

Blue jay and
monarch butterfly

Group hunters

MOST PREDATORS HUNT ALONE and fiercely defend their kills. But sometimes hunting works better in a group. Hunting in a group helps predators kill prey much bigger than themselves. The disadvantage is that they have to share the food. Many hunting groups contain less than a dozen animals, but the biggest ones—made up of soldier and army ants—can have more than a million members. Army ants cannot survive alone. Most other group-hunters are more flexible. Lions, wolves, and pelicans usually live and feed in groups, but if they have to, they can live and hunt on their own.

A BIGGER SPLASH
Gathered around a shoal of fish, brown pelicans splash noisily with their feet and wings. This keeps the fish in the center of the circle, where they are easiest to catch. White pelicans are sometimes even more methodical. Dozens of them line up side by side, and beat their wings to drive fish toward the shore.

INSECT ARMIES
In the rainforests of Central and South America, army ants surge over the forest floor for hunting. Individually, the ants are less than ½ in (15 mm) long, but a single army can contain vast numbers of them, armed with powerful jaws and potent stings. They leave the ground stripped clean of most insects, and send a steady stream of food back to their nest for the young, the worker ants, and the queen.

Centipede being captured by army ants

HERDING IN THE SEA

With their extra-large brains and keen senses, dolphins often cooperate when they hunt. Beaked dolphins, from coasts and open waters, herd fish into tight shoals known as bait balls, sometimes forcing them upward from below. Once the fish are in a bait ball, the dolphins take turns plowing through the seething mass of food. Orcas, or killer whales—the world's largest dolphins—work together to attack giant seals, sometimes tipping them from ice floes into the sea.

Dolphins herding fish into a bait ball

GRASSLAND AMBUSH

Lions are the only cats that hunt in groups, and the only ones where the males and females play different roles. Unlike hunting dogs or wolves, lionesses hunt by a carefully coordinated ambush, while the males usually stay back. The ambush may take over an hour to prepare, but the attack often lasts less than a minute before the prey is brought down. Once the prey is dead, the females eat quickly before the males arrive and displace them.

ATTACK FROM THE AIR

Huddled around a ground squirrel, a group of Harris hawks feed at the end of a successful hunt. These North American birds are very unusual, because they are the only birds of prey—or raptors—that hunt in flocks. Up to six hawks work in a squadron, forcing out prey from thick cover, or chasing animals like runners in an aerial relay race. Like most cooperative hunters, they feed in a set order, with the dominant breeding pair eating first.

African wild dogs hunting a wildebeest

RELENTLESS PURSUIT

Small and scruffy, but full of stamina, African wild dogs hunt by tirelessly running down their prey. This pack of wild dogs is pursuing a wildebeest, and the dogs will keep up the chase until the wildebeest tires and starts to falter. At this moment, the dogs move in, biting its underside and nose until it falls to the ground. After eating their fill, the wild dogs return to their den, where they regurgitate (eject contents of the stomach to the mouth) meat for the pups and any adults that stayed behind.

The waiting game

ACTIVE HUNTING CAN USE up lots of energy, and there is always a risk that it will not produce a meal. Many predators avoid this problem by using stealth to ambush their prey. Stealth-hunters are extremely varied, but have two things in common—they are patient, sometimes amazingly so, and they react almost instantly the moment prey comes within range. This way of hunting is used by some birds and mammals, but it is particularly common in cold-blooded animals, such as reptiles, amphibians, and spiders. These predators can last for days or weeks without food, but when they spot prey nearby, they are always ready to strike.

PICKING THE PLACE
Lowering itself from a flowerhead, an eyelash viper waits for visiting hummingbirds. Like most stealth-hunters, this small venomous snake lurks in places that its prey often visits. Hummingbirds hover in front of flowers as they feed, so the snake climbs into flowering plants, ready to grab its victims in midair. Eyelash vipers have a range of vivid colors, including yellow, pink, and bright green.

PATIENCE PAYS
Herons hunt by stealth, wading gently through the shallows, with their wings folded by their sides. From time to time, they stand still as statues, while they watch for fish and frogs through forward-angled eyes. If food comes nearby, the heron's hunched neck suddenly straightens, driving its daggerlike beak through the surface of the water and into its unsuspecting prey. This gray heron is catching a fish, using its wings to balance as it grasps its meal.

Tail coils up like a spring when not being used as an anchor

FIRE POWER
Anchored by a tail that is specially useful for grasping, a panther chameleon catches a grasshopper with its sticky, spring-loaded tongue. Like other chameleons, this insect-eating lizard lives and hunts off the ground, gripping twigs with its fleshy feet, and scanning its surroundings with eyes that swivel independently. A chameleon's tongue can hit its target in less than a twenty-fifth of a second. Its tip is cup-shaped and covered with mucus, which makes sure that the insect cannot escape. The panther chameleon is one of the largest of all chameleons, reaching up to 20 in (50 cm) long.

Turretlike eye is able to swivel through 180 degrees

Telescopic tongue activated by cartilage rod and special muscles

FATAL ENCOUNTER

Crocodiles are the largest predators that ambush land animals, although they live mostly in water themselves. When they are afloat, their bodies are largely hidden, except for a ridge of scales along their backs and a pair of staring eyes. This lets them swim close to the banks of rivers or lakes, where they seize animals with a sudden burst of speed. The victim is either killed instantly, or dragged underwater where it drowns. Crocodiles can grip with their teeth, but unlike mammals, they cannot chew. To eat, they bite hard and then spin around, tearing off mouthfuls of food.

Yellow color is caused by a liquid pigment secreted at the bodys surface

SNATCH SQUAD

Instead of making webs, most crab spiders lurk on flowers. Although they are small, they have strong front legs, which they hold open wide for hours on end. If an insect lands nearby, the spider's legs snap shut, helping it deliver its poisonous bite. Some crab spiders are colored brown to match bark, but ones that hunt on flowers—including this goldenrod spider—are often yellow or white.

LURKING AMONG LEAVES

For some stealth-hunters, fallen leaves provide a perfect place to hide. Their edges overlap in complex patterns, creating an ideal background for camouflage (blending into the surroundings). In the tropics, predators that lurk include some of the most dangerous snakes, as well as frogs and toads. This Amazonian horned frog is particularly aggressive, with an enormous mouth almost as wide as its body, letting it swallow many other frogs whole.

Venom and stings

HUGE NUMBERS OF PREDATORS, from jellyfish to wasps and snakes, use venom to subdue or to kill their prey. Venom is a mixture of natural poisons, and it is usually injected by something sharp, such as claws, fangs, or stings. Some kinds of venom work in less than a second, causing almost instant death. Others act more slowly, gradually paralyzing an animal's muscles so that it can no longer move or breathe. Once the prey is motionless, its fate is sealed. The predator either eats the prey on the spot, or takes the prey back to its nest to feed its young.

SPITTING VENOM
The world's most venomous snakes live in remote parts of Australia, where they cause few human fatalities because they are rarely seen. Asian cobras, on the other hand, live in densely populated areas, and cause thousands of deaths each year. Most kinds inject their venom by biting, but spitting cobras can defend themselves by spraying their venom through air. The airborne venom is harmless if it lands on dry skin, but it can cause blindness if it lands in the eyes. Spitting cobras also have a highly dangerous bite.

Gas-filled float holds up the body and acts as a sail

DEADLY TENTACLES
Buoyed up by its gas-filled float, a Portuguese man-of-war trails a cluster of stinging tentacles. Each tentacle is up to 66 ft (20 m) long, and is equipped with thousands of nematocysts, or microscopic single-celled stings. These fire at anything edible that brushes past, injecting venom through tiny harpoon-tipped threads. Each sting fires only once, but after it has discharged, a new one soon takes its place. The Portuguese man-of-war feeds mainly on fish. It usually lives in warm-water seas, and can be blown huge distances by the wind.

Pincer helps to grip prey

KILLER CLAWS
Curled around a mouse, a giant Asian centipede administers a lethal dose of venom using its poison claws. These claws are specialized legs, just behind its head, with thick bases and sharply pointed tips. Unlike millipedes, centipedes are always predatory. They hunt after dark, slipping easily through crevices and under stones. Most species are harmless to humans, but large tropical kinds—like the one shown here—can easily bite through skin, producing intense pain that takes days to fade.

STINGING INSECTS

Many insects bite, but only ants, bees, and wasps attack with stings. Bees use their stings for self-defense, but many ants and wasps use theirs to kill or paralyze their prey. Here, a spider-hunting wasp is preparing to attack a tarantula. Once the spider has been stung, its body becomes paralyzed, and the wasp drags it back to its burrow, where the spider becomes a living pantry for its young. This gruesome behavior makes sure that the wasp grubs have fresh food.

Warning ring appears only when the octopus feels threatened

Suction pad for gripping prey

WARNING SIGNS

Despite being only about 8 in (20 cm) long, the blue-ringed octopus is one of the most venomous animals in the seas. Its bite causes muscle paralysis, and can easily kill an adult human. At present, there is no antidote. Blue-ringed octopuses live on shallow rocky shores from Australia to Japan. They get their name from their bright blue rings, which pulsate vividly just before they bite, warning other animals to keep away.

Sting delivers poison

Vesicle contains poison sacs

DOUBLE TROUBLE

A scorpion has two sets of weapons—a pair of claws and a sting at the end of its tail. Scorpions use their claws to kill small animals, but for bigger prey they use the sting as well. Many scorpions—including this southern European species—are only moderately venomous to humans, but some quite small ones can kill. Scorpions hunt at night, and feed on insects and other small animals. They find their prey mainly by touch.

Hunting in the dark

WHEN DARKNESS FALLS, MANY PREDATORS stop hunting, while others come out to feed. For them, darkness is not a disadvantage. It is an ally, protecting them from their enemies as they search for their prey. Even in faint light, owls use vision to find their food. They also have superb hearing, and some can hunt by sound alone. Cats and other carnivores often use a combination of vision, hearing, and smell. Some other predators have special senses for locating prey in the dark. Bats find their food by using echolocation, while some snakes hunt by sensing body warmth. In the permanent darkness underground, some predators rely on touch and smell to catch prey.

SPLIT SHIFTS
Some predators hunt around the clock, but most work on set shifts. Diurnal predators hunt by day, and nocturnal ones by night. Crepuscular ones come out to feed at dusk, at dawn, or sometimes at both. The leopard gecko is mainly crepuscular, although it sometimes hunts through the night. Its bulging eyes work well in dim light, seeing in color when our eyes can only make out shades of gray.

Ear swivels forward to collect echoes from surroundings

ATTACK FROM ABOVE
Owls have extra-large eyes, but in complete darkness, they can often pinpoint their prey by sound alone. This skull of a Tengmalm's owl shows that its two ear cavities are of different sizes, and at different heights on its head. This lopsidedness helps the owl to fix the exact source and direction of a sound. Once it has locked on to its prey, the owl swoops down on it in complete silence.

Internal cavity of left ear is smaller and lower than right

GHOSTLY GLOW
Photographed by infrared light, a pride of lions listens for sounds of prey on the move. Their eyes have a mirrorlike layer, or tapetum, which lets them see well in dim light. This layer reflects incoming light back through their eyes, making them more sensitive. Lion hunts are most successful on dark, moonless nights as compared to the moonlit ones, since they cannot be spotted easily by their prey.

SEEING HEAT

Pythons and boas, together with rattlesnakes and their relatives, can use heat-sensitive facial pits to sense warm-blooded animals against colder backgrounds. Rattlesnakes usually have a single pit between their nostrils and their eyes, but this emerald tree boa has a line of pits on each side of the head. These help the boa judge the distance to its victim, so that it can make an accurate strike in the dark.

Row of facial pits detects infrared radiation (heat) produced by birds and mammals

SEARCHING WITH SOUND

Nearly three-quarters of all bats hunt insects by echolocation—a system that uses high-pitched pulses of sound. The pulses spread out from a bat's nose and mouth, and its ears pick up any echoes produced. As the bat speeds through the air, it builds up a picture using sound to pinpoint prey as well as any obstacles in its path. This way of hunting is remarkably precise. Bats use it to identify individual insects, and to snatch their prey from leaves or from the ground.

Tentacle

Ghost slug

ENDLESS NIGHT

Above ground, even the longest night eventually ends with dawn. But underneath the soil's surface, it is always dark. Here, many small predators stay active as long as it is moist. One of them—the ghost slug—was discovered in 2006. It feeds on earthworms, cutting them up with a ribbonlike tongue armed with microscopic toothlike denticles. Like other slugs, it has tentacles or feelers on its head, but only tiny remnants of eyes. It tracks down its prey mainly by smell.

TOUCH OF DEATH

Emerging above ground, a star-nosed mole shows off the tentacles that give it its name. It has 22 of them, arranged in a star shape around its nose, which move like tiny fingers, restlessly feeling for food. If a single tentacle touches a worm or an insect, the mole reacts with incredible speed. It identifies it almost instantly, and within a quarter of a second, swallows its prey.

Reflective layer of tissue in the eye, or tapetum lucidum, improves vision in low light

Rattlesnakes

Found only in the Americas, rattlesnakes have unique bony rattles at the end of their tails. Although generally silent, they can use their rattles to make a characteristic buzzing sound, warning other animals of a potentially lethal bite. They are slow to move unless startled, but they strike with lightning speed, lunging forward and stabbing with their fangs. There are about 30 species of rattlesnake, and they prey mainly on small mammals and birds. They range from small pygmy rattlesnakes to the highly dangerous eastern diamondback rattlesnake, which can be over 6½ ft (2 m) from head to tail. Most rattlesnakes rarely strike humans, except in self-defense.

WARNING CALL
A rattlesnake's rattle is made of bony rings at the end of its tail. The rings are hollow, and slightly loose, letting them rattle if they are given a vigorous shake. The number of rings depends on a snake's age. Newborn rattlesnakes have a single solid buttonlike structure. As the snake grows up, it adds a hollow ring each time it molts.

Nested, hollow bead of rattle is actually a modified scale

Hollow fang unfolds from roof of mouth

FOLDAWAY FANGS
A rattlesnake's fangs are at the front of its mouth and they fold flat when its mouth is closed. Just before the snake strikes, the fangs hinge forward, protected by a sheath of skin. The snake then exposes them and throws the front half of its body at its prey. With small animals, the snake injects its venom and holds on to its victim, but with large ones, it attacks and then pulls away while its venom sets to work.

Small, fixed teeth grip prey when it is being swallowed

Highly flexible joint gives jaws a wide gape

A HUNTER HATCHES

Female rattlesnakes produce soft-shelled eggs, but their eggs hatch inside their bodies, so that they give birth to live young. This way of breeding, called ovoviviparity, gives the young snakes a better chance of survival. This cascabel rattlesnake has about a dozen young per litter. From the moment they are born, the young are equipped with venom and are ready to hunt.

Young snake emerges from body opening, or cloaca

Mother's muscles contract to expel the young snake

After some time, young snake leaves its mother to hunt

RATTLESNAKE HABITATS

Rattlesnakes are common in deserts, but they are also found in many other habitats. The eastern massasauga lives in damp woodlands and swamps from Mexico northward as far as Canada. In the north of its range, it may hibernate for six months every year. Rattlesnakes also live in rainforests, in mountains, and on offshore islands in the Caribbean and the Pacific. In one species, from Santa Catalina Island in Mexico, the rattle scales fall off instead of forming the rattle, an adaptation that helps it to hunt silently in shrubs and trees.

SNAKE EATS SNAKE

Despite their venom, rattlesnakes have many enemies. These include coyotes, roadrunners, birds of prey, and kingsnakes, which are partially immune to rattlesnake venom. This kingsnake has caught a Pacific rattlesnake, and has almost finished swallowing its meal. Kingsnakes are nonpoisonous and kill their prey by constriction (squeezing). Although they are more lightly built than rattlesnakes, they have a powerful bite and grip tightly while squeezing with their coils. Other predators kill rattlesnakes using their teeth, claws, or beaks.

Rattlesnake swallowed by kingsnake

KILLING ROUTINE

For rattlesnakes, small rodents are an important food. During the day, they track them down by smell and vision, but they can also sense their body heat after dark. This rattlesnake has killed a mouse, and is maneuvering it into the right position to be swallowed. To do this, the left and right sides of the snake's jaws move independently, turning the prey so that it points head-first into its mouth.

Once the mouse is in this position, the snake's jaws then gradually draw it down the throat.

RATTLESNAKES IN ART

The beautiful patterns of rattlesnake scales are a common theme in Native American art. This basket of coiled grass stems shows a rattlesnake's diamond-shape patterning and its forked tongue. Made by the Cahuilla people, it comes from southern California. Rattlesnakes also appear as decoration on traditional pottery and on rock engravings. Many of these date back hundreds of years.

Fussy eaters

WHEN PEOPLE THINK OF PREDATORS, large meat-eaters often come to mind. But not all predators fit this description. Many are quite small animals, and some have very restricted diets—including food such as ants, eggs, or freshwater snails. In most cases, these predators are equipped with specially shaped tools—such as beaks or claws—which help them to get at their food. Some specialists spend their entire lives in the same place, while others migrate back and forth with the seasons. They also include animals such as the leatherback turtle, which can circle entire oceans in a constant quest for prey.

SNAIL SPECIALIST

The snail kite hunts in marshy places and feeds mainly on freshwater apple snails. Like all birds of prey, it has a hooked beak, but this is unusually long, with a sharply pointed tip. This kite flies slowly over the water and snatches up snails in its talons. Back at a perch, it uses its beak to prize the snail's soft body from its shell. The snail kite lives in warm parts of the Americas, reaching as far north as the Florida Everglades—where it is one of the rarest birds.

NIGHT RAID

The woodlouse spider is a wandering hunter that operates after dark. It is one of the few specialized predators of woodlice, biting through their hard exoskeletons, or body cases, with an extra-large pair of venomous fangs. In damp places, woodlice are very common, so unlike some specialized hunters, this unusual spider rarely runs short of food.

Color of the shell helps organism blend in with the sandy seabed

SPINY MEAL

Sea urchins are protected by brittle chalky spines, which keep most predators at a safe distance. However, the horned helmet shell is undeterred by this armory. Using its sucker-shaped foot, this heavyweight mollusk creeps up on an urchin, pins it down, and dissolves a hole through its body case. It then enlarges the hole using its radula—a tonguelike structure. While the helmet shell is going about this task, its foot helps to immobilize the urchin's moving spines.

JELLY-EATING GIANTS

The leatherback is one of the world's biggest specialized predators. This half-ton turtle feeds almost entirely on jellyfish, crossing the world's oceans on enormous flippers, which beat up and down like a pair of wings. Its throat has a spine that points backward, making sure that its slippery prey does not escape. Leatherbacks get their name from their shells, which are rubbery, instead of being covered with hard scutes, or bony plates.

Leatherback turtle
swimming in open ocean

*Elastic skin stretches
between scales,
letting snake's
mouth expand*

STING IN THE TAIL

Bee-eaters are colorful birds that specialize in eating bees and wasps. Using slender, curved beaks, these birds catch insects in midair and take them back to a perch to squeeze out their venom, before eating them. This bird has probably squirted out the venom from the bee's sting, tossing the bee in the air before swallowing it. In addition to hunting insects with stings, bee-eaters also eat many other kinds, from beetles to butterflies.

EGG-EATER

Eating eggs is just as predatory as eating adult prey. Many animals eat the soft eggs of fish or frogs, but this African egg-eating snake swallows birds' eggs, complete with their hard shells. Snakes cannot bite open shells—instead, the shell is broken by bony spines in the snake's neck as an egg passes down the throat. Egg-eating snakes have a keen sense of smell, which helps them to track down eggs—and avoid those that are rotten and unsafe to eat.

LAPPING IT UP

Ants and termites may be tiny, but for some animals, they make a nutritious, protein-packed food. Birds and lizards often live on this kind of diet, but the most specialized predators are mammals that lap them up with sticky tongues. The giant anteater is the largest of these mammals—it can eat over 25,000 ants or termites a day, ripping open their nests with its powerful front claws. Its tongue probes deep into the nest, flicking in and out up to 150 times a minute. Meanwhile, it sucks with its throat, sweeping up its food.

*Spine is chalky
in composition*

*Toothless snout up
to 18 in (45 cm) long*

Mantises

WITH THEIR STEALTHY MOVEMENTS and grisly habits, mantises include some of the most efficient ambush-hunters in the animal world. There are about 1,800 kinds, all armed with spiny front legs, which shoot forward to grab and skewer their prey. Most mantises are camouflaged in shades of green or brown, but some tropical species are brilliantly colored—a perfect camouflage for lurking in flowers. Mantises usually hunt among plants, but some have upright bodies, and scuttle over open ground in search of their prey. Compared to most other insects, mantises are remarkably alert to other animals, from flies to human beings. They turn their heads to follow movement, and they face danger with breathtaking defensive displays.

Mantis feeding on a hummingbird

Inward-facing spine impales prey when front leg closes

LOOK AWAY NOW
Mantises are fiercely carnivorous, and they usually feed on flying insects, such as flies, bees, and butterflies. But occasionally, some of the larger species catch much bigger prey, including tree-frogs, lizards, and birds. Here, a mantis has managed to climb aboard a hummingbird feeder, and has grabbed a hummingbird while it hovered in midair. Unlike most predators, mantises start to feed immediately, chewing through their food using strong but surprisingly small jaws. This hummingbird is already dead, but insects sometimes kick and struggle for many minutes while a mantis feeds, starting with their head.

POWER OF PRAYER
With its front legs held together, this African mantis looks like someone at prayer. This resting pose is shared by all mantises, which is why "praying mantis" is often used as their common name. Mantises have triangular heads with large compound eyes and an extremely flexible neck. By swiveling their heads, mantises can get a full view of their surroundings, letting them track any insects that fly past or land nearby.

Dead leaf mantis in startle display

FLOWER MANTISES
Deep in the forests of Borneo, this young flower mantis is perfectly disguised as an orchid flower. Its body and legs have petal-like flaps, and its abdomen is turned upward to complete the flowerlike appearance. Instead of stalking prey and staying hidden, the mantis often clings to bare stems and waits for bees to come its way. When a bee does arrive, the mantis deftly snatches it out of the air and holds it so that it cannot sting.

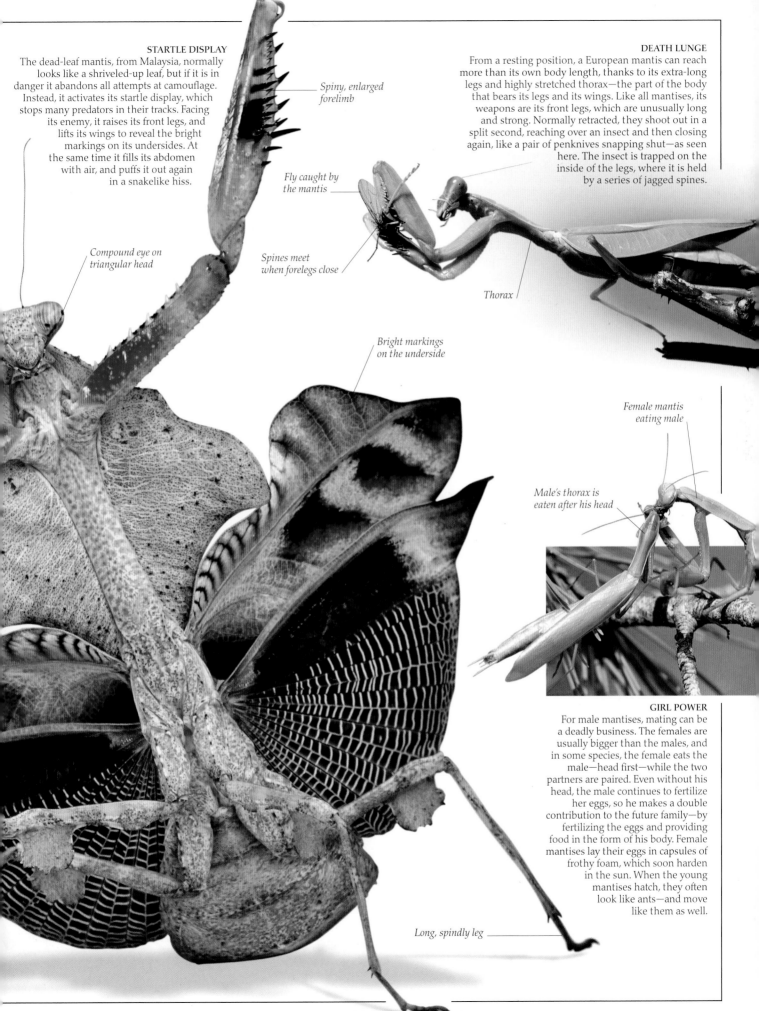

STARTLE DISPLAY
The dead-leaf mantis, from Malaysia, normally looks like a shriveled-up leaf, but if it is in danger it abandons all attempts at camouflage. Instead, it activates its startle display, which stops many predators in their tracks. Facing its enemy, it raises its front legs, and lifts its wings to reveal the bright markings on its undersides. At the same time it fills its abdomen with air, and puffs it out again in a snakelike hiss.

Spiny, enlarged forelimb

Fly caught by the mantis

Spines meet when forelegs close

Compound eye on triangular head

Bright markings on the underside

Long, spindly leg

DEATH LUNGE
From a resting position, a European mantis can reach more than its own body length, thanks to its extra-long legs and highly stretched thorax—the part of the body that bears its legs and its wings. Like all mantises, its weapons are its front legs, which are unusually long and strong. Normally retracted, they shoot out in a split second, reaching over an insect and then closing again, like a pair of penknives snapping shut—as seen here. The insect is trapped on the inside of the legs, where it is held by a series of jagged spines.

Thorax

Female mantis eating male

Male's thorax is eaten after his head

GIRL POWER
For male mantises, mating can be a deadly business. The females are usually bigger than the males, and in some species, the female eats the male—head first—while the two partners are paired. Even without his head, the male continues to fertilize her eggs, so he makes a double contribution to the future family—by fertilizing the eggs and providing food in the form of his body. Female mantises lay their eggs in capsules of frothy foam, which soon harden in the sun. When the young mantises hatch, they often look like ants—and move like them as well.

Lures and traps

VERY FEW PREDATORS—except for some unusual mammals and birds—hunt by making and using tools. But throughout the animal world, an enormous number of predators catch their prey using lures or traps. Most lures are special body parts which look temptingly like food for the prey, while traps are made by animals themselves, using natural materials, such as sand or silk. In addition to trapping prey, many double up as refuges, hiding their makers from prying eyes. Most of the animals that use lures live in fresh water or the sea. Trap-makers are exactly the opposite. They include over 40,000 kinds of spider—almost all of which hunt on land.

LUMINOUS LURES
The larvae of some fungus gnats spin threads of silk that hang from caves and fallen trees. Each thread is studded with blobs of glue. Once the threads are ready, the larvae glow softly, to lure flying insects toward their snares. In some caves in New Zealand, the larvae are so numerous that they look like stars against a night sky.

TEMPTING MORSEL
Hidden at the bottom of a lake or pond, an alligator snapping turtle holds its jaws open to reveal its tiny, bright pink tongue. The tongue wriggles just like a worm, attracting unsuspecting fish into the turtle's mouth. At this point, the turtle's jaws suddenly smash shut, cutting its prey into several pieces. This primeval-looking reptile is North America's largest freshwater turtle. It can weigh over 220 lb (100 kg).

Prey struggles to escape

Spiral strand is made of sticky silk

BENEATH THE SILK DOOR
Lined with silk, and equipped with a hinged lid, the trapdoor spider's burrow works as a trap and a hiding place. The spider normally keeps the lid shut, but after dark, it holds it slightly ajar, and spreads its front legs outside. If an insect walks past, the spider instantly reacts, throwing the lid open and rushing outside. In less than a fifth of a second, it grabs its victim and drags it underground, shutting the trap behind it. There are many kinds of trapdoor spider, and they live across the world.

ALLURING TAIL
Coiled and ready to strike, a young Mexican moccasin waves its colorful club-tipped tail. Birds are attracted by this wormlike lure, not noticing the rest of the snake, which is camouflaged against the ground. If a bird comes close enough, the lure suddenly lays flat, and the snake lunges forward to seize its prey. Mexican moccasins are venomous at all stages of their life, but only young animals have this remarkable hunting aid. It slowly disappears with age.

Microscopic image
of spinnerets
producing silk

ORB WEBS
Inching ahead cautiously, a
garden orb spider approaches a
dragonfly that has become tangled
in its web. Orb web spiders weave a
spiral of sticky strands, stretched by
long spokes attached to plants. Once
the web is complete, the spider often
waits at the far end of a special signal
spoke, waiting for telltale vibrations
showing that an insect has blundered
into its trap. When the web's working
life is over, the spider often
recycles the silk by eating
it and digesting the
protein it contains.

SILK FACTORY
Silk is an amazingly versatile material. Used
mainly by insects and spiders, it is made inside
the body. It starts out as a liquid, but turns
solid as it is squirted through nozzles called
spinnerets, and out into the air. Most spiders
can make several different kinds of silk, which
vary in strength, stickiness, and elasticity.
In addition to using silk for their webs, spiders
also use it for their egg cocoons.

*Spoke of non-sticky silk
is put in place before the
spiral strands are added*

*Bait is usually an object
that can float in water*

FISHING WITH BAIT
Some birds fish by stirring up the water, but the green heron is
unique in using bait. It picks up small objects—such as
insects, seeds, or twigs—and then drops them on the
water, while it crouches down at the water's edge.
If a fish swims close to investigate, the heron
strikes, spearing the fish with its beak. The
heron may even prepare bait, trimming
sticks so that they are the right size. This
qualifies it as a toolmaker—a rare
achievement for any predator.

Watery graves

THE STRUGGLE FOR SURVIVAL is as fierce in water as it is on land. Predators are everywhere, both in fresh water and in the seas. Some of the biggest and smallest predators eat by filtering out their food, but most hunt down their prey individually, in open water or on the seabed. Sharks and killer whales often target seals, but few fish are big enough for this kind of food. Instead, they usually target animals, including fish, smaller than themselves. Some bite off their food, like sharks do, but most suck it into their mouths—a lightning-fast movement that works by negative pressure, like a vacuum cleaner suddenly switched on. With so many predators hunting for food, growing up is highly dangerous. Many fish produce thousands or millions of young every year, but only a tiny fraction survive to be adults.

POROUS PUMPS
These bright pink sponges feed mainly on bacteria—the tiniest prey in the seas. The bodies of the sponges are shaped like vases, and they are filled with thousands of holes, or pores. Special cells lining the pores pump water through the sponge and filter out any food. Sponges are among the world's simplest animals, without internal organs or heads. Most are small, but they can be up to 6½ ft (2 m) tall and hundreds of years old.

SNAKE MIMIC
With its long body and slender fins, the spotted snake eel looks and moves very much like a snake. But it is a fish, like all eels, and has gills instead of lungs. Spotted snake eels hunt in coral reefs, killing small fish and crustaceans with powerful jaws, and swallowing food with a special second set of teeth. The spotted snake eel's markings make it look poisonous, keeping other predators away.

Tubular nostril used for detecting prey

PINCER MOVEMENT
Using its pincers, a crab carefully breaks open a sea urchin's shell. Crabs are experts at this kind of work, and many kinds are not fussy about what they eat, feeding on living animals and dead remains. There are many kinds of crab—some, such as this one, stay underwater all their lives, but others can breathe air, letting them hunt or scavenge on the shore or even further inland. However, all crabs grow up in water and have to return to it to breed.

44

CORAL CRUNCHERS

Parrotfish feed on coral polyps—the small animals that build up coral reefs. Using their beaklike jaws, they bite away the polyps, chewing each mouthful to break up the hard parts of their food. They digest the soft parts of the corals, and squirt out the waste in a stream of gritty sand. There are nearly 100 kinds of parrotfish, including some over 3 ft (1 m) long.

SHARK ATTACK!

Sharks sometimes hunt by lying in wait, or by cruising over the ocean floor, but most live in open water, tracking down their prey by sight or smell, or by sensing pressure waves or electricity (see page 18). This bull shark has caught its prey and is about to rip it apart, using a battery of several hundred teeth. Bull sharks can be highly dangerous to humans—they can hunt in lakes and rivers, as well as in the sea.

Nostril can smell blood from a great distance

ROLE PLAY

Good camouflage is vital for predators on the seabed, where there are few places to hide. The mimic octopus disguises itself by changing its color and its shape, to match the seabed, or to mimic the warning markings of poisonous animals. Here, the octopus has changed its shape to mimic a jawless fish. It hunts by squeezing through animal burrows, or by spreading itself over seabed sand, using its arms to flush out its prey.

ONE-TON MEAL

Humpback whales are some of the biggest filter-feeders on Earth. They swim through shoals of fish and krill, engulfing them with elastic mouths that can expand like a balloon. The whale then squeezes out the water, trapping food in its baleen plates—a curtain of brush-edged plates hanging from its upper jaw. Baleen is made of keratin, the same protein in hair. It grows throughout life, keeping pace with wear and tear.

Death in the deeps

MARINE BIOLOGISTS ONCE THOUGHT that noth
could survive in the deep sea. But they were w
The sea's dark depths contain some of the pl
largest predatory animals, together with ma
that feed on dead remains. Most of these hu
spend their entire lives far beneath the surfac
either in the water or on the seabed. At these
depths, the temperature is often only a few degrees
above freezing, and the pressure can be hundreds of times great
than in air. A much smaller number of predators, including sper
whales and elephant seals, dive down all the way from the surfa
to hunt. During their incredible descent, they can hold their
breath for over an hour, and they find their prey mainly by
echolocation—using high-pitched pulses of sound
that echo off objects, helping to locate
them—or by touch.

HUNTER KILLER

The sperm whale is one of the largest predators in the sea. It dives down into complete darkness, reaching depths of up to 10,000 ft (3,000 m). It uses echolocation to track down giant squid, its main food. Its enormous head contains a reservoir of oil, which helps to control its buoyancy. Beneath its head is a slender lower jaw, armed with teeth 8 in (20 cm) long—the biggest of any living predator.

FISHING FOR FOOD

In the sea's depths, female angler fish often use luminous lures to attract their prey. This lure is a modified threadlike fin spine, with a light-producing organ at its tip. If another fish swims up to inspect it, the angler suddenly opens its mouth, and sucks its prey inside. The males are much smaller than the females and do not hunt for themselves. Instead, they track down females by their scent and fasten themselves to the females' skin using their teeth. The male becomes permanently attached, fertilizing his partner's eggs, and getting food from her blood.

PATROLLING THE SEA

Throughout the world's oceans, amphipods swim over the deep seabed. Distant relatives of beachhoppers, these humpbacked crustaceans have sideways-flattened bodies, and several rows of legs that flick like oars. They have small eyes, and find their food by smell, quickly homing in on the scent of dead animals on the ocean floor. Deep-sea crustaceans also include lumbering isopods, which look like giant woodlice. Some of them are over 2 ft (60 cm) long

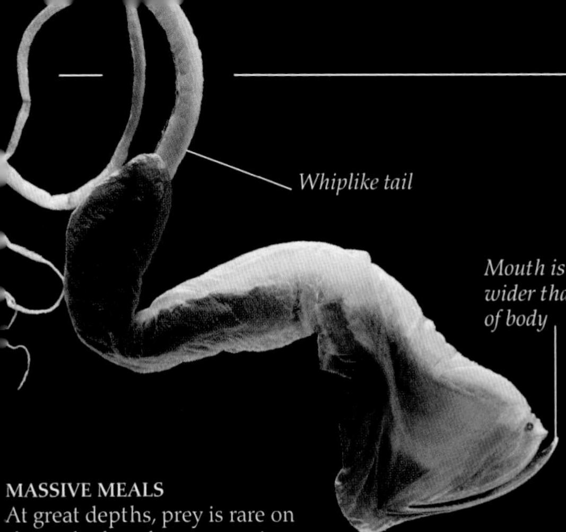

Whiplike tail

Mouth is much wider than rest of body

MASSIVE MEALS
At great depths, prey is rare on the seabed, and even rarer in open water. Hunters cannot afford to miss any chance of a meal. Many kinds—including pelican eels—have enormous mouths and elastic stomachs, giving them the best chance of swallowing any prey that they find. A pelican eel's jaw hinges near the back of its head, giving it a huge gape. Its teeth are tiny, and instead of biting, it engulfs its prey, sometimes swallowing fish that are larger than itself. Pelican eels have tails with luminous tips that attract their prey.

LIGHTS IN THE DARK
At depths beyond 820 ft (250 m), the only light is emitted by living things. Many marine predators—including this dragonfish—use light-emitting organs to attract their prey, or to make contact with their own kind. The dragonfish has a luminous barbel (whiskerlike organ), as well as light-spots, or photophores, along its body. Its stomach lining is completely black, creating a screen to prevent other predators from finding its prey, which are often luminous themselves.

Gaping jaw helps swallow prey nearly half fish's own size

Light-emitting barbel contains luciferin—a chemical that produces light but very little heat

EIGHT-LEGGED GIANTS
Deep-sea predators can be much larger than their relatives from shallow water. These massive hunters include giant sea spiders, or pycnogonids, with a legspan of nearly 3 ft (1 m)—50 times bigger than many sea spiders of coral reefs. The deep-sea species feed on worms and other soft-bodied animals, attacking them with mouthparts that pierce skin and suck up body fluids. Even in giant sea spiders, there is very little space for internal organs—a reason why the digestive system reaches into the legs.

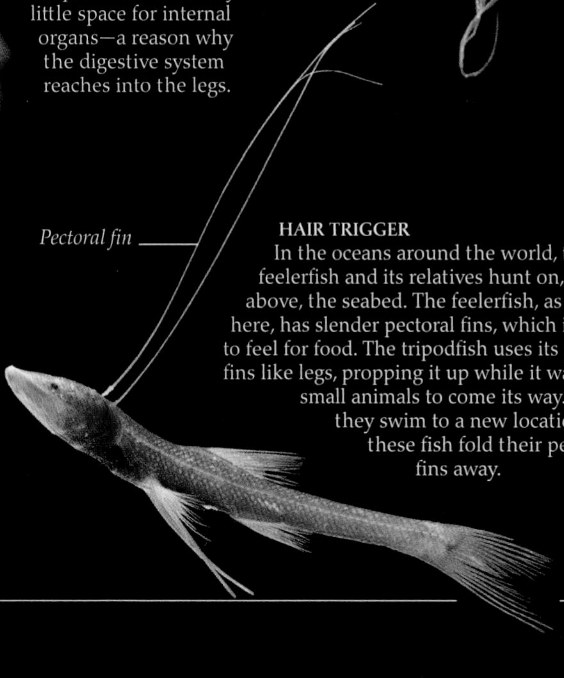

Pectoral fin

HAIR TRIGGER
In the oceans around the world, the feelerfish and its relatives hunt on, or just above, the seabed. The feelerfish, as shown here, has slender pectoral fins, which it uses to feel for food. The tripodfish uses its pectoral fins like legs, propping it up while it waits for small animals to come its way. When they swim to a new location, both these fish fold their pectoral fins away.

Squid and cuttlefish

WITH THEIR SUPERB EYESIGHT and large brains, squid and cuttlefish are some of the most remarkable predators in the seas. Like octopuses, they are mollusks, and have eight sucker-bearing arms. They also have two longer tentacles, sometimes armed with hooks, which shoot out to catch their prey. Except for these hooks, their only hard parts are a parrotlike beak, tiny teeth, and internal skeletons known as pens and cuttlebones. Squid and cuttlefish speed through the water using jet propulsion, or swim on rippling fins. Cuttlefish usually feed in shallow water for fish and crabs, but squid can be found both near the surface and in the darkest depths, feeding on all kinds of prey. Many squid are small and slim, but giant squid are the world's largest invertebrates, measuring over 43 ft (13 m) long.

MYTHS AND MONSTERS
Ever since people first went to sea there have been persistent tales of monsters with sucker-bearing arms. This early engraving shows a giant octopus attacking a sailing ship. The first confirmed sighting of a giant squid dates back to 1861, when one attacked a steamship off the Canary Islands.

SHRIMP HYPNOTIST
Cuttlefish are experts at the art of camouflage. With their flat bodies and stubby arms, they move stealthily over the seabed, changing appearance to match its texture as well as color. This species—the broadclub cuttlefish from the Indo-Pacific—feeds mainly on shrimp, and uses rapid color changes to hypnotize and lure its prey. Once the prey is within range, the cuttlefish suddenly extends its tentacles, grabbing and pulling the victim within reach of its arms and jaws.

Eight arms held together in a cone

Broadclub cuttlefish searching for food

Bands of dark color pulse rhythmically along body and arms, mesmerizing prey

Beak stabs prey

KILLER BEAKS
Surrounded by the base of their arms, squid and cuttlefish have a poisonous beak that they use to kill their prey. This beak is of a Humboldt squid, from the eastern Pacific Ocean. Made of chitin—the same substance as in insect skeletons—the beak has a complex system of hinges and is over 2 in (5 cm) long. The beaks of giant squid can be as big as a fist. The beaks are sometimes found in the stomachs of sperm whales, which hunt squid in the deep sea.

OPEN-WATER SQUID
In the open water, fast-moving squid often live in large shoals, feeding on fish and planktonic animals. These swordtip squid from the Sea of Japan swim tail-first, squirting out a jet of water from a body cavity, called the mantle, and beating their winglike fins. Their large eyes have mirrorlike linings, and their skin can change color rapidly, matching their mood or the sea.

Shrimp caught in the tentacles of a cuttlefish

DEEP-SEA VAMPIRES

Found in the sea's dark depths, tiny vampire squid are a small and ancient group of animals, with eight arms joined by webbing, and slender filaments instead of tentacles. They live at depths of over 6,600 ft (2,000 m), and hunt by swimming slowly, and emitting light for luring potential prey that brushes past. The squid shown here has adopted a defensive posture that makes it look bigger than it really is.

Web of skin connects the arms

Egg shell is translucent

THE NEXT GENERATION

Squid and cuttlefish breed by mating and laying eggs, often gathering in large numbers when conditions are right. Here, a female inshore opalescent squid is adding her egg capsules to ones that other females have already laid. Squid eggs have thin translucent shells, and they hatch to produce young squid that look like miniature versions of their parents. The parents, meanwhile, die of exhaustion, leaving the young to grow up on their own.

Skin contains chromatophores that can shrink or expand to alter cuttlefish's color

COLOR CODING

Feeding on a shrimp, this common cuttlefish shows the pigmented spots, or chromatophores, which it uses to change color. Each chromatophore is a single cell, containing an elastic sac of colored chemical, or pigment. Around the cell are small muscles and nerves, which can make the pigment sac change shape. In a fraction of a second, the cuttlefish can alter the chromatophores all over its body, sending waves of color rippling down its back. This ability helps the cuttlefish in camouflage and for communicating while mating. It can even make its left side look different to its right.

Scavengers

SOME PREDATORS EAT ONLY FOOD they have killed, but many also eat dead remains of animals. In nature, dead remains never stay in one piece for long. Lured by sight and smell, a succession of scavengers moves in and eats them. The menu is huge, and often changes with the time of year. At one extreme, it often features swarms of insects, which have finished their life cycles and died. At the other, it can feature the corpses of huge animals such as elephants, seals, and whales. Thanks to scavengers, all of these are eventually cleared away, while smaller organisms, called decomposers, return the final fragments to the soil. Two kinds of animals are involved in scavenging work. Some, like vultures, scavenge but rarely actually kill. Competing with them are predators, from hyenas to polar bears. Despite being hunters, they also eat dead animals, including carcasses that may be days or weeks old.

SWITCHING ROLES
Wolverines are famous for their large appetites, and scavenge all kinds of animal food, including leftovers from wolf kills. These animals are also capable hunters, preying on animals such as elk and caribou, which are several times their own size. For wolverines, the height of the scavenging season is in late winter, when many animals die. Winter is also a good time for hunting, because the wolverine's flat paws work best on frozen snow.

Vertebrae (backbone) of prey stripped of flesh

DOUBLING UP
Australia's wedge-tailed eagle is the continent's largest bird of prey. In a land without scavenging vultures, this eagle often behaves like one, feeding on the remains of big animals. This bird may feed alone, but it is not unusual to see several gathered around a kangaroo corpse. Many other large eagles share the wedge-tailed eagle's scavenging streak—one of the best known is the bald eagle, America's national bird.

Spotted hyena and vultures feeding off a carcass

UNMISSABLE OPPORTUNITIES
On a coast in Norway, this polar bear is feeding on the beached remains of a minke whale. In addition to targeting the whale's meat, the polar bear feasts on its blubber—the thick layer of body fat beneath the whale's skin. Blubber is packed with energy, making it a perfect fuel for a predator that lives in icy conditions. Minke whales can weigh up to 15½ tons (14 metric tons), so there is enough food here to sustain many polar bears for some weeks.

GOING, GOING, GONE

Large carcasses can attract a succession of predators and scavengers, each feeding on different parts of the remains. Vultures usually concentrate on soft parts of the flesh, but spotted hyenas swallow practically anything they can tear off and swallow, including teeth, bones, and pieces of dried-out skin. They digest all this with their powerful stomach acids—a talent that few other scavengers can match.

BONE-BREAKER

Vultures are good at tearing open soft flesh, but their beaks are too weak to crush bones. The bearded vulture, or lammergeier, carries bones into the air and drops them on rocks. The force of the impact smashes them open, letting the vulture feed on the soft marrow inside. On coasts, other scavenging birds—such as gulls and terns—use a similar technique to feed on hard-shelled mollusks and crabs.

DAYLIGHT ROBBERY

Instead of hunting their own food, some animals steal it from other predators. Known as kleptoparasites—meaning thief parasites—they include small spiders that lurk on other spiders' webs, and also many seabirds. While skuas and frigatebirds chase their victims through the air, this black-headed gull is ambushing a puffin—for food—as the puffin returns to its nest. Its beak is laden with sand-eels—tiny fish destined for its chicks.

Allies and opportunists

IN THE OCEANS, CLEANER SHRIMP pick their way over all kinds of fish, and even walk inside their mouths. It looks incredibly dangerous, but it is just one of many partnerships involving predators and other animals. Some of these partnerships are permanent, and the two partners are never seen on their own. Others—like the ones involving cleaner shrimp—last for a limited time, after which the partners go their separate ways. Often, both animals benefit, but sometimes the predator is left empty-handed, or worse off than before.

Tiny pincer collects pieces of food

CLEANER AT WORK
Dwarfed by a coral grouper, a cleaner shrimp searches its client for parasites and specks of leftover food. While the shrimp goes about its work, the grouper keeps perfectly still, even letting the shrimp examine its teeth and gills. This cleaning service keeps the grouper in good condition, while the shrimp benefits by eating whatever it finds. Cleaner shrimp are often brilliantly colored, which helps them to be seen. Each one operates from a prominent cleaning station, where fish line up and wait their turn. In coral reefs, some small fish also offer cleaning services themselves.

NIT PICKING
On Española Island, in the Galapagos, a mockingbird lands on a marine iguana, and picks ticks and dead scales from its skin. The mockingbird's long beak is ideal for this kind of task, although unlike a cleaner shrimp, it does not only live by cleaning—it also attacks living prey. Española Island mockingbirds have a strong curiosity for anything that might be edible, from insects to tourists' shoes.

UNEASY ALLIES
In North America's grasslands, coyotes and badgers normally avoid each other, because they are both well armed with strong jaws and sharp teeth. But occasionally, a coyote and a badger temporarily join forces to hunt ground squirrels and other rodents. The coyote is good at chasing rodents, while the badger is better equipped for digging them out of their burrows. However, there is no sharing—in this partnership, each animal eats whatever it kills.

PORTABLE PROTECTION
Crabs and sea anemones often form long-term partnerships. Predators leave the crabs alone because they carry sea anemones that are armed with stings. In turn, crabs often drop food as they eat, producing leftovers that the anemones can use. Some crabs carry anemones on their backs, but this boxer crab holds them in its claws, like a pair of gloves. Because its claws are full, it uses its first pair of walking legs to tear up its food.

A PATIENT WAIT

Lining up for a chance to feed, three black-backed jackals watch a spotted hyena at its kill. Even though there are several of them, they keep a careful distance, because the hyena is a lethal threat. The hyena tolerates their presence as it finishes off most of the carcass. When it leaves, the jackals quickly move in, and eat up any food that is left.

FREE RIDE

Remoras, or sharksuckers, fasten themselves to sharks, whales, and other large animals, using their unique pad-shaped dorsal fins. If their host drops any food, the remora quickly swims out to catch it, before fastening itself back in place. This lemon shark is carrying nearly a dozen of these fish, clustered mainly underneath its body. The remoras get easy food and a free ride, but contribute little in return.

Sea anemone is held in a crab's claw for protection from predators

Fang remains hidden in the lower jaw

UNKIND CUTS

Peering out from its burrow in a reef, a false cleaner fish waits for unsuspecting clients. It looks almost exactly like a true cleaner fish, and it displays its services like one as well. But if another fish presents itself to be cleaned, the false cleaner shows its true nature. It bites off pieces of skin with its pointed fangs, before its duped client realizes this and speeds away.

Storing food

COMPARED TO HUMANS, MANY predators have an amazing capacity for food. A leopard can eat 22 lb (10 kg) of meat in one sitting, while spiders can eat half of their weight in a day. But food soon attracts scavengers, as well as other predators that steal hard-won kills. Rather than lose out, some predators protect their food by hiding it, or by putting it in places that scavengers cannot reach. Leopards sometimes drag their food into trees, but most predators bury their food underground. Days or weeks later, they track down their stores, or caches, by remembering landmarks, or by using sight and smell. Their memories can be phenomenal. Foxes, for example, can remember the exact position of more than 50 caches, creating an emergency food store in hard times.

Remains of a beetle that the shrike has eaten

Beetle wing case impaled by sharp thorn

Lizard impaled through the back

SPIKED
Shrikes, or butcherbirds, catch small animals and then spike them on thorns in special food stores called larders. In addition to storing food, shrike larders help to preserve it, because small animals quickly dry out in the sun. Once fully dry, they do not rot, so they stay edible for weeks. Here, a red-backed shrike is eating a lizard that it has caught. The thorn holds the lizard firmly in place, while the bird tears up its food with its hooked beak.

READY WRAPPED
Sitting on its web, this female wasp spider is surrounded by insects that she has caught and wrapped in shrouds of silk. She will use this stored food in the days ahead, when she needs extra protein to make her eggs. Food stores like these sometimes attract smaller spiders, which climb aboard the web. The owner does not notice as they stealthily help themselves to some of the prey.

Prey wedged in fork of tree to keep it stable

Recently caught grasshopper wrapped in silk

Leg winds silk around prey to create a close-fitting shroud

WEIGHT LIFTER
Leopards hide food in long grass, but where there is no cover, they drag it high into trees. Their strength is exceptional, even for predators of their size. Gripping its prey in its teeth, this adult male has hauled a springbok up a thorn tree. The carcass may weigh up to 88 lb (40 kg), but the leopard may even tackle animals twice this size. Once the body of the dead prey is safely off the ground, the leopard either wedges it in a fork, or flops it over a branch. It then begins to feed, untroubled by scavengers and lions on the ground below.

LIVE STOCKPILE

European moles feed on earthworms—prey that is hard to find when the ground is frozen or dry. To survive during winter and summer, they stockpile worms in underground stores. Normally, captured worms would wriggle away, so the mole carefully processes them first. It bites each worm in the head, which paralyzes but does not kill it. It then ties its prey in a knot, using its teeth and its paws. The worm can now be added to the stockpile, where it stays fresh until it is needed.

BURIED TREASURES

Digging with its front paws, a red fox buries some surplus food in a hole. When food is plentiful, a red fox can dig dozens of these caches a night. Each one contains a single small animal or piece of meat. After the fox has covered up the cache, it marks it with urine, helping it to find the cache when it is hungry. This kind of behavior is common in all dogs and foxes. In the far north, Arctic foxes use caches to survive the extreme winter cold.

Parasites

Nearly every animal on earth carries parasites, living on or inside its body. A parasite feeds on its host animal, or sometimes on the animal's semidigested food. Many parasites are small or microscopic, but the biggest include parasitic worms over 33 ft (10 m) long. Some parasites have just one kind of host animal, but many have complicated life cycles involving two or three different kinds of host animal. Unlike predators, true parasites, such as fleas and tapeworms, often weaken their hosts but do not normally kill them. Parasitoids—such as potter wasps—live in a different way. They capture and paralyze other animals, using them as living food stores for their grubs (larvae). By the time the grubs are fully grown, their host is dying or dead.

Microscopic image of cat flea

ALL ABOARD
Fleas are tiny wingless insects that suck blood from mammals and birds. They jump aboard by kicking with their powerful back legs, which can send them somersaulting over 12 in (30 cm) through the air. Unlike most insects, their bodies are flattened from side to side, helping them to slip through feathers and fur. There are over 2,000 kinds of these common parasites. Some are restricted to a single kind of host, but many—including the cat flea—live on a range of animals. Fleas can spread diseases.

INSIDE JOB
Hugely magnified, a tapeworm's head, or scolex, shows the hooks and suckers that keep it in place. Tapeworms live in the intestines of animals with backbones. Their bodies are long and flat, with dozens or even hundreds of separate segments. Each segment absorbs food from its surroundings, and also has its own reproductive system, which makes enormous numbers of eggs. Tapeworms grow from a point just behind their heads, producing new segments in a steady stream. At the same time, the oldest segments break off from the end of the tapeworm. These carry off the eggs to infect new hosts.

BREAKOUT
This catalpa sphinx moth caterpillar is surrounded by dozens of tiny cocoons. Each one has been spun by a braconid wasp grub. Together, the grubs have grown up inside the caterpillar, using it as food. In the next part of their life cycle, the grubs will turn into adult wasps, breaking out of the cocoons to find mates and produce eggs themselves. This way of life may seem gruesome, but it is extremely common in the insect world. There are over 100,000 species of braconid wasp, and nearly all are parasitoids.

Round mouth without jaws

Concentric rows of teeth

UNHEALTHY ATTACHMENT
Animals with backbones are often attacked by parasites, but few are parasites themselves. Lampreys are jawless fish and most of them are parasites. Most kinds spend their early lives in fresh water, where they live by filtering out particles of food. As adults, they migrate to the sea, changing shape to develop suckerlike mouths armed with sharp teeth. Lampreys use these to attach themselves to fish at sea, rasping away their flesh and drinking their blood. If a lamprey clings on long enough, it can kill its host.

Sacculina, *a parasitic barnacle that attaches to crabs*

GOING TO EXTREMES
Internal parasites include animals with extreme adaptations for very specialized ways of life. Shore crabs can be attacked by a parasitic barnacle, called *Sacculina*, which spreads through its host like the roots of a plant, reaching the tips of the crab's legs and claws. The parasite gets all its food from the crab. From the outside, the only sign of *Sacculina* is a swelling on the crab's underside. This produces the eggs that infect other crabs.

*Nest made
of mud and
saliva*

Paralyzed caterpillar

FOOD FOR THE POT
Female potter wasps make
special nurseries for their
grubs, using a mixture of
saliva and mud. The wasp
shapes the mud into a pot,
and then lays a single egg
inside. Next, she stocks the pot
with a paralyzed caterpillar, before
sealing it with a lid. After the egg hatches, the wasp
grub feeds on the caterpillar. It then pupates,
turning into an adult wasp before breaking out
of its home. Like most wasps, adult potter
wasps feed on nectar and sweet fruit.

*Sucker prevents
tapeworm from
being dislodged
during intestinal
movement*

SLAVE TRADE
Slave-making ants attack other ants' nests, and carry
pupae—ants that are partly developed—back to their
own colony. In this unusual kind of parasitism, the
pupae turn into slaves when they become adults.
From then on, they devote their time to running
the nest, and looking after the slave-makers' young.
In the raid shown here, black slave-making ants are
attacking red ants in their underground nest.
The pupae being carried off are white.

*Hook helps attach to
intestinal walls of host*

*Reed warbler
feeding cuckoo
fledgling*

BROOD PARASITES
Instead of attacking
other animals directly,
brood parasites trick
them into bringing up
their young. Here, a reed
warbler has been tricked into
raising a common cuckoo. It is
still feeding the cuckoo after it
has left the nest, even though
the young bird is twice its own
size. Brood parasites include
many other egg-laying animals,
from cowbirds to bumblebees.

Feeding on blood

BLOOD IS PACKED WITH NUTRIENTS, which makes it an almost perfect food. Lots of animals feed on it, and some eat nothing else. Most full-time blood-feeders are insects, but blood-feeders also include many other animals, from leeches and ticks to vampire bats. Unlike typical predators, blood-feeders are usually much smaller than their prey, and they have special mouthparts for piercing or cutting open skin. While they are feeding, they use special chemicals to stop the blood from clotting, and once their meal is over, most depart as stealthily as they arrive. Blood-feeders hardly ever kill, but they can weaken animals and spread dangerous diseases.

A TASTE FOR BLOOD
The Maasai people, from Kenya and northern Tanzania, are among the few human societies who traditionally drink liquid blood. They are seminomadic cattle herders, and cattle blood makes up an important part of their diet, together with meat and milk. In many other parts of the world, blood is a traditional ingredient in preserved meat products.

DEEP CUTS
Most blood-feeding insects have painless bites, even though they often make the skin itch. Horseflies and their relatives are much less delicate, because the females slice through skin with powerful, jagged jaws. They often circle around horses and other large mammals, landing on their necks, where they are difficult to dislodge. Female horseflies have heavy bodies and large iridescent eyes. The males are often smaller, and feed at flowers.

CARRYING DISEASES
Landing on a bird called an I'iwi, or Hawaiian honeycreeper, a mosquito takes a meal from the bare skin around the bird's eye. The mosquito's mouthparts work like a hypodermic syringe (hollow needle used for injections), protected by a folding lower lip that acts as a guide. While the mosquito feeds, it injects saliva—carrying special chemicals called anticoagulants—to keep the blood flowing. Mosquitoes sometimes spread blood-borne parasites, including ones that cause avian (bird) malaria. Hawaiian honeycreepers are particularly at risk from this disease. Malaria-carrying mosquitoes were accidentally introduced on the Hawaiian Islands early in the 19th century. Since then, about 20 species of honeycreeper have become extinct.

BAT ATTACK
Vampire bats attack large mammals and birds, landing near their prey and then scuttling toward them on all fours. Their saliva contains an anesthetic that stops the victim from being woken by a bite, and an anticoagulant, called draculin, which keeps the blood flowing while the bats lap it up. Vampire bats attack after dark.

Leech attached to a goldfish

VAMPIRE BIRDS
Many birds pick parasites from larger animals, but some have also evolved a taste for blood. In the Galapagos Islands, the vampire finch feeds mainly on seeds and insects, but it also pecks at large seabirds, feeding on the blood that flows from their wounds. Here, a number of vampire finches are attacking a Nazca booby, which is particularly tame and makes no attempt to chase the finches away since it does not perceive these birds as a threat. In addition to drinking blood, vampire finches also break open eggs.

TIME TO FEAST
Found on land and in water, leeches are distant relatives of earthworms. They have a sucker at each end of the body. The rear sucker works like an anchor, while the front one contains sharp mouthparts that can pierce skin to suck blood. Land-based leeches often find prey by waiting on plants, but aquatic kinds can swim. This freshwater leech is exploring a goldfish's scales for the best place to feed. It will drop off when its meal is complete.

Conical beak has sharp edges

Illustration showing a 16th-century treatment chamber

GET THE BLOOD FLOWING
Leeches were once widely used in medicine, because it was thought that blood letting (removing infected blood) helped to treat disease. This medieval engraving shows patients waiting in a treatment room, where medicinal leeches were kept in earthenware jars. Even today, leeches are sometimes used after surgery to stimulate blood flow to skin grafts.

Cannibals

W HEN FOOD IS SCARCE, many animals will eat their own kind. Most of them are predators, but animal cannibals include omnivores (animals that eat both plants and animals), and plant-eaters, too. Cannibalism usually happens when animals are on the brink of starvation, but it can be a normal part of their life cycles. The range of animal cannibals is enormous. On land, cannibals include crocodiles, lizards, amphibians, and insects and slugs. Cannibalism is also common in freshwater and marine animals, from lobsters to killer whales. Victims of cannibalism can be the old or the young, and animals that have met with accidents and died. More sinister still, it sometimes happens before animals are even born.

Egg sac

THINNING THE RANKS
With its egg sac still attached to its body, this sand tiger shark is a confirmed cannibal, even though it has just been born. Female sand tiger sharks produce up to 80 eggs, which hatch inside their bodies. A deadly struggle then follows, as the largest embryo sharks eat the smallest. By the time the young are ready to be born—about 16 months later—only one, or sometimes two, are left.

EATING THE DEAD
Dining with their pincers, two Sally lightfoot crabs pick over the dead body of a third. Crabs are omnivorous, and remains like this can provide them with a useful source of food. This behavior is common in many other predators and omnivores, on land and in water. Slugs and crickets, for example, often eat the remains of their own kind that have been squashed on roads. But not all wait until their food is dead—flock-forming birds, such as starlings, sometimes eat the disabled and the sick.

Bulging eye spots the slightest movement, even when prey is well camouflaged

Multihinged jaws shoot out from under the head, and retract to haul in prey

KILLER MALE
When food is short, many carnivorous animals prey on the young of their own species. Polar bear cubs are particularly vulnerable in late summer, when their mothers are waiting to take them hunting on the frozen sea. Their mothers defend them fiercely, but adult males are huge, hungry, and aggressive, and without any family ties. The remains seen here are those of a cub killed by the male.

FROM HUNTER TO HUNTED
Dragonflies spend the first part of their lives in fresh water, as predatory nymphs with powerful multihinged jaws. Hunting by stealth, they often catch and eat each other—in some species, over half of their food consists of their own kind. Here, a nymph has caught one slightly smaller than itself, and is starting on its meal.

Female black widow spider

Male black widow spider

FINAL APPROACH
For male spiders, mating can be dangerous, because the females are usually much larger, and sometimes have a cannibalistic streak. To protect himself, a male black widow wraps his partner in silk, which makes it much harder for her to treat him as a meal. Other species are not so lucky. A male Australian redback spider actually encourages the female to eat him, by positioning himself in front of her jaws. By becoming food, he helps her to produce her eggs.

DEADLY TAKEOVER
In most kinds of cannibalism, animals kill for food. But cannibalism also happens when adults kill to assert control. If a lion pride is taken over by a new group of males, they often kill all the existing cubs, so that the future ones are all their own. This adult male has caught a year-old cub. Its chances of survival are slim, because it is on its own. Adult females, or lionesses, sometimes defend their cubs, but they put their own lives at risk because they are smaller than the adult males.

Young Komodo dragon

SAFETY OFF THE GROUND
At over 10 ft (3 m) long, Komodo dragons are the largest lizards in the world. Adults have no natural enemies, but they are cannibalistic predators and scavengers, eating each other's eggs and young. To survive, young dragons head into the trees after hatching, where they feed mainly on birds and eggs. The adults are too big and heavy to climb, so the young are safe until they are large enough to defend themselves on the ground.

Green hunters

PLANTS DON'T NEED FOOD, but they do need simple chemical nutrients to grow. Most get these nutrients from the soil. But where the soil is poor or waterlogged, carnivorous or predatory plants use insects and animals, catching them with strangely shaped traps—which are mainly highly specialized leaves. Some traps lure animals into pools of fluid where they drown. Others work by snapping shut or by suddenly changing shape, sucking animals inside. Once the victims are dead, the plants slowly digest the nutrients they contain. Fungi also include predators, particularly in damp places and in the soil. Most work stealthily by infecting prey and then slowly growing inside them.

Droplet of sweet-smelling glue attracts insects

STUCK FAST
Found in wet places, sundews use sticky hairs to trap insects landing on their leaves. This great sundew has caught a fly, its hairs bending over to make sure that its prey cannot escape. While the insect struggles to get away, the leaf tip bends as well, giving the sundew an even better hold. It takes the leaf at least a week to digest the fly's nutrients. Afterward, the leaf unrolls again, revealing the insect's lifeless husk.

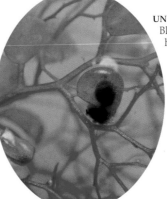

UNDERWATER TRAPS
Bladderworts grow in lakes and ponds and have tiny capsules, or bladders, attached to their feathery underwater stems. Each bladder has a hinged door, attached to a set of trigger hairs. In this one, the hairs have been touched by a tiny animal. The bladder's door has suddenly opened and then closed, imprisoning the dark shape—the prey—inside.

Trapped fly being digested inside closed leaf

Trapped fly attempting to escape

SNAPPING SHUT
The Venus flytrap has some of the fastest reactions in the entire plant world. This green predator from North America has leaves with two hinged lobes, edged by long points that look like teeth. To hunt, the trap is held open, inviting insects to land. If an insect does settle on the trap, it brushes special trigger hairs. Almost instantly, the trap begins to close. The lobes hinge together, and in less than a tenth of a second, the teeth start to interlock, sealing the insect inside.

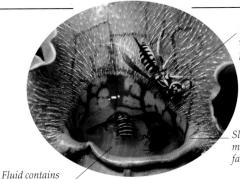

Wasp about to fall into pitcher

Fluid contains enzymes that digest prey

American pitcher plant

Slippery rim makes insect fall inside

Plant looks like a lidded pitcher

PITCHER PLANTS

Two different families of plants use pitcher-shaped traps to catch their prey. North American pitcher plants have clusters of tall, narrow pitchers with slippery rims. The pitchers attract insects with the scent of sugary nectar—when an insect lands to feed, it falls in. In southern and Southeast Asia, tropical pitcher plants catch animals with elaborate traps at the ends of their leaves. Shaped like pitchers with lids, their traps are the biggest of all carnivorous plants—some are large enough to catch small lizards and mammals.

Tropical pitcher plant

FAMILY ALBUM

For over two centuries, tropical pitcher plants have fascinated botanists and plant-hunters. There are over a hundred species, together with many cultivated hybrids. The German artist and biologist Ernst Haeckel painted some of the most eye-catching kinds in this famous family portrait. It appeared in his hugely successful book *Artforms in Nature*, which was published in the early 1900s.

Toothlike edge on lobe

Trigger hair on inner surface of leaf lobe

PREDATORY FUNGI

Seen through a microscope, life and death plays out among a few particles of soil. The grooved objects are tiny nematode worms, which have been caught by the threads of a soil-dwelling fungus. The fungus catches its prey with ring-shaped traps, which suddenly expand if a worm wriggles through them. In less than a fiftieth of a second, the worm is caught, and ready to be digested.

ATTACK FROM WITHIN

Insects are attacked by predatory fungi at all stages of their lives. Here, a fungus has attacked a moth pupa or chrysalis (the stage between a larva and an adult), and has grown a fruiting body that scatters its microscopic spores. The fungus feeds by spreading through the pupa while it is on the ground, and its spores help it to spread from one insect to the next. Predatory fungi help to control the populations of many insects, such as flies, grasshoppers, and locusts. Without the fungi, these organisms would be even more common than now.

Fruiting body grows out of pupa to scatter spores into air

Food chains

FOOD CHAINS BEGIN WITH PRODUCERS, such as plants. Unlike animals, these collect the Sun's energy and use it to make food. Their energy is transferred when they are eaten by consumers, the first animals in any food chain. Energy moves on again when consumers are eaten by predators, and whenever predators eat each other. The food chains end with a top predator.

African savanna

In tropical grassland, grasses are the main producers. They are eaten by grasshoppers, which are hunted by scorpions. Meerkats feed on scorpions, which in turn, are attacked by martial eagles, which end the chain.

Grass

Grasshopper

South American tropical rainforest

Rainforest orchids provide food for bees. Motmots eat bees, but are hunted by tree boas. These are attacked by tegus, particularly when they are young. Jaguars are the top predators in this food chain.

Orchid

Bee

Motmot

Amazonian tree boa

European temperate lake

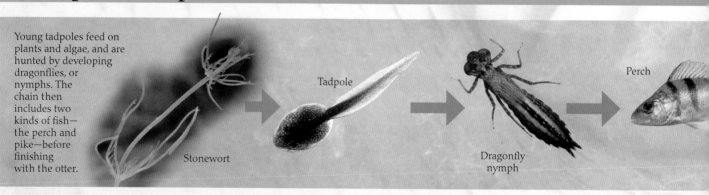

Young tadpoles feed on plants and algae, and are hunted by developing dragonflies, or nymphs. The chain then includes two kinds of fish— the perch and pike—before finishing with the otter.

Stonewort

Tadpole

Dragonfly nymph

Perch

Pacific Ocean

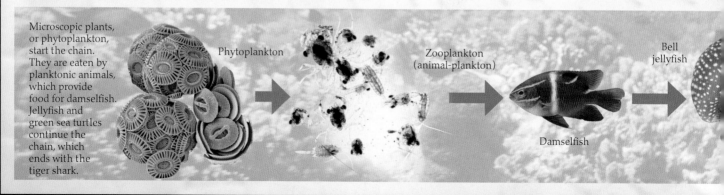

Microscopic plants, or phytoplankton, start the chain. They are eaten by planktonic animals, which provide food for damselfish. Jellyfish and green sea turtles continue the chain, which ends with the tiger shark.

Phytoplankton

Zooplankton (animal-plankton)

Damselfish

Bell jellyfish

Imperial
scorpion

Meerkat

Martial
eagle

Tegu

Jaguar

European
otter

Pike

Green sea
turtle

Tiger
shark

Animal records

FROM THE BLUE WHALE to the wandering albatross, it is the predators who hold many of the most prominent records in the animal world. The biggest animal is more than 50,000 times longer than the smallest, and the most poisonous can kill animals hundreds of times its own size. Record-breaking predators live all over the planet, from rainforests to polar seas. In some habitats, they have been closely studied. In others—particularly the deep ocean—scientists are discovering more every year.

Largest predator on Earth

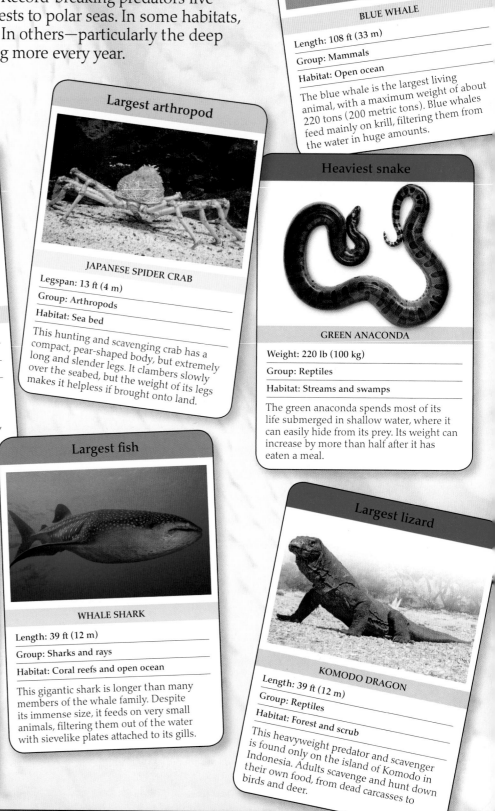

BLUE WHALE

Length: 108 ft (33 m)

Group: Mammals

Habitat: Open ocean

The blue whale is the largest living animal, with a maximum weight of about 220 tons (200 metric tons). Blue whales feed mainly on krill, filtering them from the water in huge amounts.

Largest arthropod

JAPANESE SPIDER CRAB

Legspan: 13 ft (4 m)

Group: Arthropods

Habitat: Sea bed

This hunting and scavenging crab has a compact, pear-shaped body, but extremely long and slender legs. It clambers slowly over the seabed, but the weight of its legs makes it helpless if brought onto land.

Largest predator on land

POLAR BEAR

Weight: 1,540 lb (700 kg)

Group: Mammals

Habitat: Arctic coasts and seas

The polar bear is the heaviest terrestrial predator. It spends summer on land, but hunts on sea ice in winter, feeding mainly on seals. The brown bear is a close second, rivaling it in weight.

Heaviest snake

GREEN ANACONDA

Weight: 220 lb (100 kg)

Group: Reptiles

Habitat: Streams and swamps

The green anaconda spends most of its life submerged in shallow water, where it can easily hide from its prey. Its weight can increase by more than half after it has eaten a meal.

Largest frog

GOLIATH FROG

Weight: 7¾ lb (3.5 kg)

Group: Amphibians

Habitat: Rivers and streams

Found in west Africa, the Goliath frog is a strong swimmer and spends most of its life in fast-flowing water. It feeds on a wide range of animals, including other frogs and freshwater crabs.

Largest fish

WHALE SHARK

Length: 39 ft (12 m)

Group: Sharks and rays

Habitat: Coral reefs and open ocean

This gigantic shark is longer than many members of the whale family. Despite its immense size, it feeds on very small animals, filtering them out of the water with sievelike plates attached to its gills.

Largest lizard

KOMODO DRAGON

Length: 39 ft (12 m)

Group: Reptiles

Habitat: Forest and scrub

This heavyweight predator and scavenger is found only on the island of Komodo in Indonesia. Adults scavenge and hunt down their own food, from dead carcasses to birds and deer.

Largest spider

GOLIATH BIRD-EATING SPIDER

Legspan: 11 in (28 cm)

Group: Arachnids

Habitat: Rainforests

This huge spider spends the day in a burrow and comes out at night to hunt. It finds its prey by touch and eats anything it can overpower, including insects, lizards, and roosting birds.

Fastest predator in water

SAILFISH

Speed: 68 mph (110 kph)

Group: Bony fish

Habitat: Open ocean

Swimming at top speed, the sailfish slashes its way through shoals of fish and then eats its dead or injured prey. Its body is packed with swimming muscles, which have an extra-rich blood supply.

Fastest predator on land

CHEETAH

Speed: 70 mph (112 kph)

Group: Mammals

Habitat: Savanna and grassland

Speeding up rapidly from a standing start, the cheetah could overtake most cars. It uses these bursts of speed to catch antelope and other mammals. But it can maintain the speed only for short spans of time.

Largest living reptile

SALTWATER CROCODILE

Length: 20 ft (6 m)

Group: Reptiles

Habitat: Rivers, coasts, and shallow seas

Ranging from India to Australia, young saltwater crocodiles eat fish and even insects, but adults are capable of killing fully grown water buffalo. This aggressive reptile causes many human fatalities each year.

Predator with largest wingspan

WANDERING ALBATROSS

Wingspan: 11½ ft (3.5 m)

Group: Birds

Habitat: Open ocean

The wandering albatross soars over the stormy waters of the southern ocean, snatching animals from the surface. Its long beak has a sharply hooked tip, which stops prey from slipping out of its grasp.

Most toxic fish

WHITE-SPOTTED PUFFERFISH

Lethality: Toxins could kill 25 people

Group: Bony fish

Habitat: Coral reefs

The white-spotted puffer stores a virulent poison in parts of its body, particularly its liver. It feeds on hard-shelled animals, such as mollusks and crustaceans, and uses its poison to protect itself against predators.

Smallest predatory animal

ROTIFERS

Minimum length: 0.002 in (0.05 mm)

Group: Rotifers

Habitat: Water and damp places

Many predatory animals are too small to be seen with the naked eye. Rotifers are among the tiniest—some kinds are smaller than some bacteria. They use tiny moving hairs to capture food.

Most venomous invertebrate

BOX JELLYFISH

Lethality: Toxins could kill 50 people

Group: Cnidarians

Habitat: Coasts and open sea

Box jellies are much more venomous than other jellyfish, and also stronger swimmers. Their trailing tentacles can be fatal for anyone who accidentally touches them with bare skin.

Most poisonous amphibian

GOLDEN POISON-DART FROG

Lethality: Toxins could kill 10 people

Group: Amphibians

Habitat: Tropical rainforest

This thumb-sized predator feeds on insects and other small animals and uses poison to defend itself. The poison oozes through glands in its skin.

Predators in danger

Humans can make it difficult for animals to survive, but predators are often at greatest risk. Top predators are naturally rare and vulnerable, and they may be targeted by poachers and trophy hunters. Further threats come from habitat changes, such as deforestation. An international body called the IUCN (International Union for the Conservation of Nature) determines the risk of extinction of each endangered species and puts animal species into categories, such as "critically endangered." This is an important first step in saving these species.

KAUAI CAVE WOLF SPIDER

Total numbers: Unknown

Status: Endangered

Major threats: This rare Hawaiian spider lives only in lava caves. Development of nearby land causes erosion and pesticide runoff inside the caves, endangering it.

Conservation action: The spider's habitat is now officially protected. In 2005, young spiders were seen for the first time in 30 years.

TIGER

Total numbers: 3,000–5,000

Status: Endangered

Major threats: Once found across the whole of Asia, the tiger's range and numbers have collapsed dramatically, mainly as a result of deforestation and hunting. At one time, there were eight subspecies. Three of them—the Caspian, Javan, and Sumatran tigers—have already become extinct.

Conservation action: The Global Tiger Initiative is coordinating international action to save this majestic predator.

PHILIPPINE EAGLE

Total numbers: 200–500

Status: Critically endangered

Major threats: One of the world's largest birds of prey, this eagle has been decimated by the destruction of its rainforest habitat in the Philippines, and also by illegal shooting and trapping.

Conservation action: Officially protected since the 1970s, the eagle is now being helped by forest conservation and captive breeding programs.

SCALLOPED HAMMERHEAD SHARK

Total numbers: Unknown

Status: Endangered

Major threats: Young hammerheads are threatened by accidental capture in fishing nets, while humans deliberately target the adults for their fins. Adults gather in large schools, making them easy to find.

Conservation action: Fishing for shark fins is now banned in some countries. Other countries are likely to follow soon.

LEATHERBACK TURTLE

Total numbers: 50,000–100,000

Status: Critically endangered

Major threats: Egg harvesting threatens young turtles, while adults are accidentally caught in fishing nets. Another threat is the development of breeding beaches as tourist resorts.

Conservation action: Protection of nests aims to stem this turtle's steep decline.

DUSKY GROUPER

Total numbers: Unknown

Status: Endangered

Major threats: This top predator has a slow growth rate and a long reproductive cycle, which means its population cannot recover quickly from overfishing. Males do not breed until they are about 12 years old, and because they stand their ground to defend their territory, they are an easy catch for spearfishers.

Conservation action: Spearfishing bans can help this species.

GOLDEN MANTELLA

Total numbers: Unknown, but probably less than 1,000

Status: Critically endangered

Major threats: One of the world's rarest frogs, this tiny amphibian lives in just a few patches of rainforest in western Madagascar. Most of its habitat has been destroyed, putting it on the brink of extinction.

Conservation action: Protection in national parks will help.

NORTHERN QUOLL

Total numbers: Less than 10,000

Status: Endangered

Major threats: This small Australian marsupial is threatened by a variety of introduced species—particularly cats and poisonous cane toads—and also by forest fires.

Conservation action: Habitat conservation and measures to combat introduced species helps.

PROTECTING PREDATORS

Using a handheld microwave scanner, a scientist checks the identity tag of a Kemp's ridley turtle on a nesting beach in Mexico. Tags like these can be tracked by satellite, helping biologists to see how far animals migrate, where they breed, and also how many still remain. Predators are also protected in other ways. These include captive breeding programs, which produce young animals that can be released into the wild, and also international laws against cross-border trade in live animals and their body parts, such as fur.

Glossary

Antennae of a common wasp

ANTENNA (plural, **ANTENNAE**)
Paired feelers on an animal's head. Antennae are used to smell or touch, and some can be used to hear. Some small water animals also use antennae like oars when they swim.

BALEEN
A substance found in large whales that filters small animals from seawater. Baleen has frayed edges and hangs in vertical plates from a whale's upper jaw.

BIOLUMINESCENCE
The production of light by living things. Some animals make light themselves, but many use bacteria to produce light for them.

BROOD PARASITE
An animal that tricks others into raising its young. Brood parasites include common cuckoos and many other birds, and also some kinds of bee.

Camouflage in soft coral crab

CAMOUFLAGE
Colors and patterns on an animal's body that help it to blend in with its background.

CANNIBALISM
Eating of one animal by another of its own kind. In cannibalism, the predator is usually older than its prey.

CARNASSIALS
Bladelike teeth in the cheek, found in many mammalian carnivores. Carnassials work like shears, cutting through meat and sometimes cracking open bones.

CARNIVORE
Any meat-eating predator. In a narrower sense, it means a member of the order Carnivora—a group of mammals that includes dogs, wolves, foxes, weasels, bears, and cats. These animals share the same body plan.

CHROMATOPHORE
A skin cell that contains a drop of pigment, or chemical color. Some chromatophores can alter the shape of the drop, helping to change an animal's overall color.

CLOTTING
The process that makes blood turn solid when a wound begins to heal or when blood is exposed to air.

COCOON
A silk case made by some insects and spiders. Cocoons protect animals or their eggs.

COLD-BLOODED
Properly termed ectothermic, having a body temperature that varies according to the conditions in the environment. Most animals, except for birds and mammals, are cold-blooded.

COMPOUND EYE
In insects and other invertebrates, an eye that is divided into many compartments, each with its own lens. By working together, the compartments produce an overall image.

CONSTRICTOR
A snake that squeezes its prey to death, stopping it from breathing.

DORSAL FIN
A fin on an animal's back.

ECHOLOCATION
A way of sensing objects by producing high-frequency sound and detecting the echoes from those objects. Echolocation is used by two main groups of predator—insect-eating bats, and dolphins and other toothed whales.

ECTOPARASITE
A parasite that lives and feeds on the outside of a host animal's body.

ECTOTHERMIC
See COLD-BLOODED.

EMBRYO
An animal in the very early stages of development.

ENDOPARASITE
A parasite that lives and feeds inside its host animal's body.

ENDOTHERMIC
See WARM-BLOODED.

ENZYME
A protein that speeds up a chemical reaction. Enzymes are essential to life, because many reactions in living organisms would be too slow without them.

Falcon fledgling

EVOLUTION
Natural changes that occur over many generations, affecting the way living things look and live, creating variety of life on Earth. Changes are controlled mainly by the process of natural selection, by which the features that help a life form to survive are passed on to its offspring.

FANG
A large tooth that is shaped to bite deeply, either to grip or to inject venom.

FILTER-FEEDER
An animal that filters its food out of water, instead of chasing prey one by one.

FLEDGLING
A young bird that is not fully feathered and not yet able to fly.

FOOD CACHE
A secret store of food hidden by an animal for use at a later time.

FOOD CHAIN
A food pathway that shows how energy and nutrients pass from one species to another. Food chains often start with plants, which use the energy in sunlight. Some of this energy is then passed on when animals eat plants, or each other.

Molt in
red snake

FOSSIL
The remains of something that was once alive, preserved in rock, or simply traces of past life. Most fossils preserve hard body parts, such as shells and bones.

HABITAT
The surroundings that an animal needs to find food and to breed. Some animals can live in a range of habitats, but most live in a single one.

HERBIVORE
An animal that feeds entirely on plants, or plant-based food.

HIBERNATE
Spending winter in a deep sleep, with the body's normal processes slowed down. During hibernation, an animal lives on its stores of body fat so that it does not have to look for food at a difficult time of year.

Brown bear, an omnivore

INSTINCT
A pattern of behavior that is already in place when an animal is born.

INVERTEBRATE
An animal without a backbone, or any kind of bony skeleton. Invertebrates are often small, but they make up by far the majority of animal species on Earth.

JACOBSON'S ORGAN
An organ of smell in the roof of the mouth. Many land animals, such as snakes and some mammals, use it to taste the air, helping them to find prey or others of their own kind.

LARVA (plural, LARVAE)
The young stage of an animal that looks completely different from the adult stage, changing shape as the animal grows up. Caterpillars and tadpoles are examples of larvae.

NATURAL SELECTION
One of the main driving forces behind evolution. Natural selection acts on individuals within a population. It happens when living things that are not fit enough to survive in an environment die out. The ones that are left pass on their features to their offspring and so on, and these features gradually become more widespread.

MOLT
Shedding of hair, skin, or the body's outer case. In animals with a body case, the old case is replaced by a new one so that the animal can grow.

NEMATOCYST
A microscopic cell armed with a stinging thread. Nematocysts are found in cnidarians, which include corals, sea anemones, and jellyfish.

NYMPH
A young insect that resembles its parents and changes shape gradually as it grows up. Nymphs do not have working wings or reproductive systems.

OMNIVORE
An animal that eats a wide range of animal- and plant-based food.

OWL PELLET
A hard lump containing indigestible pieces of food, such as fur and bones, regurgitated by owls. Some other birds also do this.

PARASITE
A living thing that lives on or inside another, called its host, using it for food. Normally, parasites do not kill their hosts.

PARASITOID
An animal that starts life as a parasite and ends up by eating and killing its host. Most parasitoids are small insects.

PLANKTON
Small living things—including animals, algae, and single-celled living organisms—that swim and drift in the surface waters of oceans and in lakes.

POLYP
A simple animal with a tubelike shape and one body opening surrounded by tentacles. Sea anemones, corals, and young jellyfish share this body form.

RADULA
A ribbonlike feeding organ found in many mollusks. Its rows of tiny, tooth-shaped structures called denticles scrape food into the mouth.

REGURGITATE
To eject partly digested food back through the mouth.

SCAVENGER
An animal that feeds on dead remains, usually of other animals or their food.

SPECIES
A group of similar living things that can breed with each other to produce young like themselves.

Sting

Scorpion

STING
A body part that is specially shaped for injecting venom. Stinging animals include bees, ants, wasps, scorpions, and jellyfish.

STOOP
The high-speed dive used by some birds to attack their prey in midair.

TALON
In predatory birds, a long curved claw that is used for killing and for grasping prey.

TAPETUM
A mirrorlike layer at the back of an animal's eye that reflects light back through light-sensing cells. Found in many nocturnal animals, it makes the eyes more sensitive when the light is faint.

VENOM
A mixture of substances that can injure or kill. To work, venom usually has to be injected through stings or fangs.

VERTEBRATE
Any animal with a backbone, including mammals, birds, reptiles, amphibians, and all fish except hagfish. Most vertebrates also have a complete skeleton made of bone.

WARM-BLOODED
Properly called endothermic, having a warm and stable body temperature despite the conditions in the environment. Endothermic animals include birds and mammals.

Index

Acknowledgments

Dorling Kindersley would like to thank:
Caitlin Doyle for proofreading and Helen Peters for the index.

The publisher would like to thank the following for their kind permission to reproduce their photographs:

(Key: a-above; b/g-background; b-below/bottom; bl-below left; br-below right; c-center; cl-center left; cr-center right; cla-center left above; clb-center left below; cra-center right above; crb-center right below; f-far; fbl-far below left; fbr-far below right; fcl-far center left; fcr-far center right; ftl-far top left; ftr-far top right; l-left; r-right; t-top; tl-top left; tr-top right.)

Alamy Images: Anaspides Photography - Iain D. Williams 61tr, Peter Arnold Inc 57cr, Arterra Picture Library 52cr, ArteSub 48br, blickwinkel 62c, Scott Camazine 4br, 22c, 63tl, Jane Gould 67cr, David Hosking 60b, imagebroker 18tl, 50cr, Images of Africa Photobank 29cr, Juniors Bildarchiv 66bl, Nature Picture Library 41cr, North Wind Picture Archives 48tl, Michael Patrick O'Neill 39tr, Wolfgang Pölzer 69tr, Laura Romin & Larry Dalton 61crb, tbkmedia.de 13cl, Glyn Thomas 51cr, Masa Ushioda 53c, WaterFrame 48bl, Dave Watts 2cl, 54tl, The Wildlife Studio 29cl; **Amgueddfa Cymru–National Museum Wales:** 35cr; **Ardea:** Steve Downer 49tl, Chris Knights 57br, Gavin Parsons 44tl, George Reszeter 22tr, Duncan Usher 54bl, M Watson 25b, Alan Weaving 57tr, Jim Zipp 24cr, 25tr, 25c; **Aurora Photos:** Robert Caputo 51b; **The Bridgeman Art Library:** 37bc, Private

Collection/Photo © Heini Schneebeli 24tl; **Corbis:** Ron Austing 3tl, 25fbr, Bettmann 59br, Frank Burek 34tl, Michael Callan; Frank Lane Picture Agency 9tl, Clouds Hill Imaging 56tl, DLILLC 65cra, Richard du Toit; Gallo Images 65tr, Martin Harvey 64-65b/g, 66-67b/g, 68-69b/g, 70-71b/g, Eric and David Hosking 25br, 69c, Don Johnston/All Canada Photos 31bl, Steve Kaufman 12cla, Dennis Kunkel Microscopy, Inc./Visuals Unlimited, Inc. 43tl, Bruno Levy 17b, Joe McDonald 13br, Momatiuk - Eastcott 45b, Arthur Morris 38tl, David A Northcott 65cla, John Pitcher/Design Pics 52cl, Jeffrey L Rotman 12bl, 36cra, 37tl, 37tc, 37tr, 37cr, 53t, Rykoff Collection 2tl, 25cr, Denis Scott 66tr, Will Troyer/Visuals Unlimited, Inc. 3c, 67cl, Visuals Unlimited 70tl, Visuals Unlimited/David Fleetham 65bl, Stuart Westmorland 65br, W. Wisniewski 67tr, Norbert Wu/Science Faction 49tr, Solvin Zankl/Visuals Unlimited 70b; **Adrian Dancy:** 24bl; **Dorling Kindersley:** Courtesy of The National Birds of Prey Center, Gloucestershire 70cr, Courtesy of the Natural History Museum, London 2br, 12cr, Courtesy of the Natural History Museum, London 21cr, Courtesy of the Weymouth Sea Life 4cr, 33tl, Courtesy the Natural History Museum, London 4clb, 35cb, © David Peart 64-65b, Tim Shepard, Oxford Scientific Films 20c, Jerry Young 66cl; **FLPA:** Chris Mattison 31br, Michael & Patricia Fogden/Minden Pictures 42tr, Elliott Neep 8b, Ingo Arndt/Minden Pictures 18r, L Lee Rue 58tl, Gary K Smith 43c, Winfried Wisniewski 55t; **Getty Images:** AFP 27t, Tom Brakefield 17tr, Minden Pictures/Matthias Breiter 9tr, De Agostini 44cr, Michael DeFreitas 11bl, Digital Vision/Justin Lewis 66bc, Digital Zoo 65tc, Minden Pictures/Michael Durham 23cl, Don Farrall 27cr, Flickr/Alexander Safanov 29t, Jeff Foott 18bl, Gary Bell 67bc, National Geographic/Chris Johns 58bl, Martin Harvey 24cl, Image Source 71bl, Darryl Leniuk 15br, Ethan Meleg 27fcr, Minden Pictures/

Flip Nicklin 6cl, Minden Pictures/Fred Bavendam 8bl, Minden Pictures/Jan van Arkel/Foto Natura 4b, 7cb, 19br, 28t, 30b, 44bl, 56cl, 62tl, 67bl, Minden Pictures/Mark Moffett 33tr, Minden Pictures/Mitsuaki Iwago 17t, Minden Pictures/Norbert Wu 4cla, 7bl, 46cl, 47tl, 47br, Minden Pictures/Tui de Roy 42bl, 43br, 58r, Oxford Scientific/John Mitchell 2crb, 21tl, Eastcott Momatiuk 67c, National Geographic/Bianca Lavies 36b, National Geographic/Klaus Nigge 26c, 50l, 68br, National Geographic/Nick Norman 6cla, National Geographic/Paul Sutherland 16l, 31t, Oxford Scientific/Werner Bollmann 20-21b, Minden Pictures/Gerry Ellis 13bl, Purestock 69bl, Sabine Scheckel 14tl, Steve Gschmeissner/SPL 6br, 64bl, Hans Strand 61l, Stuart Westmorland 5tr, 19tr, J. Sneesby/B. Wilkins 14b; **Hans Hillewaert:** 56br; imagequestmarine.com: Mark Conlin/V&W 46tl, Peter Parks 32cr; **naturepl.com:** Dave Bevan 59tr, Mark Bowler 26bl, Stephen Dalton 38tr, Damschen/ARCO 30cl, Bruce Davidson 29br, 37cl, Martin Dohrn 28b, 34-35b, Doug Perrine 23tr, 69br, Georgette Douwma 19crb, 48cl, Nick Gordon 16cr, Barry Mansell 59tl, Bence Mate 11r, Dietmar Nill 34r, Pete Oxford 39br, Michael Pitts 61br, Michael Richards/John Downer 32tl, David Shale 65cb, 46bl, 47tr, Lynn M Stone 50t, Andrew Walmsley 12tl, Doc White 7t, Wild Wonders of Europe/Elander 51tr, Wild Wonders of Europe/Varesvu 39cr, Rod Williams 42br, Solvin Zankl 26tl; **NHPA/Photoshot:** Daniel Heuclin 61ca, Oceans Image 53cr, Alan Williams 8t; **Photolibrary:** age fotostock 21tr, Juniors Bildarchiv 20tl, Bios 39cl, Sylvain Cordier 55br, Bios/Michel & Christine Denis-Huot 45tl, Bios/Régis Cavignaux 25bc, Bios/Yann Hubert 45tl, cuboimages/Paolo Galperti 63tr, Garden Picture Library/Brigitte Thomas 62b, All Canada

Photos/Wayne Lynch 19ca, Tsuneo Nakamura 52-53b, OSF/Elliott Neep 65crb, R Andrew Odum 42tl, OSF/Berndt Fischer 1, 25tl, OSF/David B Fleetham 66c, OSF/Joaquin Gutierrez Acha 33b, OSF/Alex Hibbert 10cr, OSF/Colin Milkins 10b, OSF/Splashdown Direct 52tl, OSF/Tony Allen 10tl, Hans Pfletschinger 61tl, Phototake Science/Dennis Kunkel 57tl, Fritz Poelking 22b, Wolfgang Poelzer 49b, Jeffrey L. Rotman 23br, 60tl, Gérard Soury 46tl, Still Pictures/JUAN PABLO MOREIRAS/FFI 4tr, 30tl; **Science Photo Library:** Biophoto Associates 63cr, Gregory Dimijian 35tr, Eye of Science 6cr, 11tl, 45tr, 56bl, 63tc, Tom McHugh 4tl, 32cl, Matt Meadows 63bl, Rod Planck 35cl; **SeaPics.com:** Nat Sumanatemeya 38b, 45cr; **Igor Siwanowicz:** 40c, 40bl, 41l; **Gordon C. Smith, U.S. Fish and Wildlife Service:** 68tl; **Tom Vaughan FeVa Fotos:** 40tl; **Visuals Unlimited, Inc.:** 10cl

Jacket: Front: Corbis: image100 b; **Getty Images:** Oliver Anlauf tr, Kendall McMinimy tl; **Photolibrary:** OSF / Berndt Fischer tc; **Back: Alamy Images:** Scott Camazine c; **Ardea:** Jim Zipp ; **Corbis:** David Northcott br; **naturepl.com:** Dietmar Nill cr; **Photolibrary:** Juniors Bildarchiv bl

Wallchart: Alamy Images: Scott Camazine br, The Wildlife Studio; **Corbis:** Don Johnston/All Canada Photos crb, Momatiuk—Eastcott cra, John Pitcher/Design Pics c/ (coyote); **FLPA:** Elliott Neep b; **Getty Images:** Michael DeFreitas cl, Minden Pictures/Jan Van Arkel/Foto Natura crb/ (English sundew), National Geographic/Bianca Lavies clb, National Geographic/Paul, Natoional Geographic/Paul Sutherland tl; **Science Photo Library:** Michael Patrick O'Neill tr

All other images © Dorling Kindersley
For further information see: www.dkimages.com